The Stolen Goddess

The Kaphtu Trilogy:
Book Two

By

Richard Purtill

ISBN: 1-4107-5275-5 (e-book)
ISBN: 1-4107-5276-3 (Paperback)

This book is printed on acid free paper.

1stBooks – rev. 06/17/03

Original edition published by DAW Books

Cover art by Don Maitz.

For more about the Kaphtu Trilogy and other works by
Richard Purtill,
visit our official website at
http://www.alivingdog.com.

This book is dedicated to the people who helped
or urged me bring it back into print:

Lilia Castle
Gord Wilson
Don Maitz
and
Lucy Watters

Chapter One
THE OLYMPIAN

I can always tell an Olympian, even if he chooses to walk among us mortals in disguise, so I knew that the young man was one of the Immortals as soon as he entered the wineshop, a sailors' gathering place on the docks at Amnisos. I know the Olympians because I am used to them; of my mother's three best friends two were mortal women who had become Olympians and one was a goddess who had become a mortal woman. The tale of their adventures had been my favorite story as a child and my love for those stories had brought me here to the chief port of the land of Kaphtu.

It had started when my mother was a young girl in Athens. She had been chosen as one of the seven maidens who, along with seven youths, were sent to Kaphtu by Aegeus, King of Athens, after M'nos, the Sea King, had defeated him. The war had started when Andaroko, son of M'nos, had been killed by a bull in Athens. According to my mother, this was probably the fault of Andaroko. He had been trained as a bull-leaper in the great Dance which the Kaphtui dance in honor of Posudi, the sea god, although when he was killed by the bull it was not in the Dance. He was drunk and trying to show off his prowess to the Athenians. Perhaps Aegeus encouraged him for his own ends, but my mother said that Andaroko had deserved his fate by making a game of the Dance, which is a serious and holy thing.

M'nos, at any rate, had blamed Aegeus and had gathered the great fleet of Kaphtu for an attack on

Attika and Athens, its capital. When military force produced a stalemate, M'nos called on the Gods Below, with whom he had already begun meddling. No one knows what they did to Aegeus, or threatened him with, but Aegeus soon gave in and granted the demands of M'nos.

The vengeance of M'nos was as much a blasphemy of the Dance as his son's drunken daring had been. He planned to take seven youths and seven maidens of royal, or at least noble, Athenian blood every year and pretend to train them for the Dance. Without the skill of the Kaphtui Dancers and without anyone with the power to control the bull, he expected them to be killed as his son had been killed. It did not seem to bother him that Posudi might be offended by this misuse of the Dance for vengeance. Posudi was the Earthshaker as well as the Lord of the Sea and the palace of M'nos at N'sos might well have been shaken down about his ears if his plot had succeeded and blood was shed on the Court of the Dance.

The plans of M'nos were defeated mainly by one of the Athenians sent in the Tribute of Fourteen, a girl called Chryseis whose real name was Britomartis. She made friends first with P'sero, the captain of the ship that brought the Fourteen to Kaphtu, and then with Ariadne, daughter of M'nos. Between them, Ariadne and Britomartis managed to get the Athenians properly trained as Dancers, and Britomartis discovered that she herself had the power over animals which would enable her to act as the Tauromath, the Dancer who controls the bull with his or her mind so that the other

Dancers may dance with him, leap over his back and roll under his hoofs without being killed.

To increase her power, Britomartis had walked the Path, the mysterious passage between worlds that can lead either to the Lower World or to the Bright Land, the home of the gods. Britomartis found herself in the Bright Land and able to live there without being destroyed, as most mortals would be. As she learned later, this was because her mother was an Olympian, the goddess called Aphea by the Danaans but Britomartis by the Kaphtui. Aphea had fallen in love with Lykos, a master craftsman, who was a younger brother of Aegeus, King of Athens. They had lived together in peace for eight years, a cycle which has some mysterious significance for the Olympians. After eight years, Aphea was forced to return to the Bright Land, leaving her daughter, Britomartis, with Lykos, who was living quietly as a poor craftsmain the city his brother ruled. Seven years later Britomartis was chosen along with my mother and the others as part of the Tribute of Fourteen and came to Kaphtu.

Britomartis and Ariadne, with powerful help from the Bright Land, defeated the plans of M'nos and afterward shielded the land of Kaphtu from the worst effects of the Great Wave, which ravaged the coast of Kaphtu when the fire-mountain on Dariapana exploded. Then they helped the Kaphtui fight off the invasion of Argive sea raiders which followed the destruction made by the Great Wave. In the course of these events, Ariadne had discovered that her real father was not M'nos but Posudi and that she, too, could live in the Bright Land.

Ariadne and Britomartis trained and protected the first two groups of Athenian Dancers. The third group was led by Theseus, heir of King Aegeus, who had already met Britomartis on a reconnaisance of Kaphtu. With the help of Ariadne's friend Daedalus, the Athenian craftsman who had lived in Kaphtu for many years, Theseus almost persuaded Ariadne to marry him and unite the kingdoms of Kaphtu and Attika against the Argive threat. M'nos had reacted by sending Theseus down the Path to be killed by Astariano, the monstrous being who was the son of P'sephae, the wife of M'nos and one of Those Below. With the aid of Ariadne and Daedalus, Theseus defeated Astariano and fled with Ariadne. But on the island of Naxos, where their ship had been blown by a storm, Ariadne was claimed as a bride by Dionysus, son of Zeus, and Theseus had to content himself with Ariadne's sister, Ph'dare.

Ariadne, however, had vanished from the ken of mortals and was thought to be dead, so Theseus's marriage with Ph'dare made him the heir of M'nos, since in Kaphtu the husband of the Ariadne, the oldest daughter of the current M'nos, is the next M'nos. When M'nos pursued Daedalus, who had fled to Sicily and there went down into the Lower World, Theseus became King of Kaphtu, as he had become King of Athens on the death Aegeus. I knew, though, that Theseus had never been comfortable with the name or style of M'nos and largely governed Kaphtu by viceroys sent from Athens.

My mother, Alceme, had been the friend and ally of both Britomartis and Ariadne, but before the Great

Wave she and my father, N'suto, had left Kaphtu for the kingdom of Karia on the Asian mainland, along with my grandmother Riamare and my grandfather (as I thought then) P'sero, captain of the ship that had brought my mother to Kaphtu. Karia was ruled by Riadamantes, estranged brother of M'nos, and he was presently joined here by his old friend Lykos. When Britomartis persuaded the Olympians to accept her in place of her mother, Aphea was permitted to join Lykos in Karia and there to live out her life as a mortal woman. For most of my life, Karia had been ruled by Riadamantes, Lykos and Aphea. P'sero, and after his death my father, N'suto, were Councillors of the Kingdom, probably the richest and most influential people in the kingdom after the royal three.

My mother went her own way, her blonde loveliness very little changed, to my eyes at least, from my first memories of her. She could have been powerful and influential in the kingdom as my grandmother Riamare was, but she cared very little for such things. She had been not just an ordinary Dancer but one of the Leapers and had done the head leap over the horns of the bull. She was fiercely devoted to my father and to us her children and ran the household with ease and efficiency, but she kept a private life which included keeping herself strong and healthy. She went off on mysterious journeys from time to time, though she always seemed to be there when we needed her.

I will never forget my mingled admiration and boyish embarrassment at what happened one day in the harbor near our house. On one of my father's ships the tackle had become fouled near the top of a high mast. Someone light would have to climb the mast and clear the ropes. I was only a child and none of the men unloading the ship were young and agile enough. My father was about to try it himself but my mother, who had brought me down to see the unloading, stopped him. "You'll break the mast, love," she said with affectionate derision. "Here, hold the boy." Before my father could reply, she had stripped her Kaphtui-style flounced skirt and was up the mast like a monkey from Nubia. She wore a kilt like a man's under her skirt, an old Dancer's habit, and she was still in Dancer's trim. When she came down after clearing the tangle she was scarcely even breathing hard.

My father was annoyed at her showing her legs to the whole harbor, as he put it. A Dancer's kilt covers very little. But she soon brought him around as she always did. Neither she nor my grandmother was a woman to be ruled by men except by her own consent. A stranger might have thought they ruled their husbands, but both P'sero and my father were men with their own kind of strength, and their wives respected them even if they sometimes outmaneuvered them for their own good as my mother had outmaneuvered my father by climbing the mast.

Karians are uncertain about the role of women; they inherited the patriarchal attitude of the Danaan immigrants as well as the uneasy equality with memories of matriarchy of the Kaphtui immigrants. The native people of the land are of the same stock as the people of Kaphtu, which is why they accepted Riadamantes as ruler when he came here with his followers from Kaphtu after he quarreled with M'nos. The official religion of Karia is the cult of Zeus— under the title Laburiantos, 'he of the double axe"— and the double axe of Kaphtu is the symbol of equalitv between god and goddess, man and woman. The Danaan immigrants had private cults of the Olympians, and many of the Kaphtui and native Karians worshipped the Mother or some of the Olympians under their Kaphtui names.

My knowledge of the Olympians was not gained in temples. Very often there were mysterious visitors at the palace or even at our home overlooking the harbor, visitors with whom only my mother, Aphea and Lykos seemed entirely at ease. We children loved them, but we soon realized that adults outside of our family often did not see our visitors at all or saw them differently from the way we did. I think what impressed me most as a child was that my formidable grandmother Riamare, who feared no mortal, feared these visitors.

The most frequent visitor was Britomartis, who was my playmate from the time I started to walk and who soon became "Aunt Brit" to me. She looked then, as she looks now, like a girl on the threshold of becoming a woman, but even as a child I think I realized that she did not grow older as other girls did. She was fond of children, whom she treated as equals without patronizing baby talk and was the perfect older sister or young aunt. We rarely saw any other side of her personality when we were children.

Ariadne was a less frequent visitor. Though her face and figure were not much older than Britomartis's, she seemed older, for she was a wife and mother. She often had a baby with her and for years it was the same baby, for time runs more slowly in the land of the Olympians; her visits, at long intervals to us, seemed to be only a short time apart to her. No one could have been sweeter or kinder but there always seemed to me to be something of Olympian strangeness about her. That only gave her enchantment in my eyes; my first adolescent infatuation was for Ariadne.

More rarely yet, Dionysus, whom we all called Dion, came with Ariadne. He could descend to our level at any age and led us children in wild romps which left us exhausted but happy. There was always something dangerous and untamed about him, which of course was part of his attractiveness. We never feared for ourselves but sometimes we held our breath when some adult seemed to annoy him. He was at his most human with Ariadne, whom he obviously adored.

All of the Olympians are dangerous, of course, and a mortal associates with them at his own peril. They have tremendous power and do not always remember the fragility of mortals. Aphea had been an Olympian herself and understood them. Lykos had married a goddess and seen his daughter become a goddess in turn, but his lack of fear was due to his scale of values; he feared only becoming unjust and held that no one can make one unjust except oneself. My mother had a kind of strength that was linked to less attractive qualities, a sort of inner toughness that could seem like selfishness and a self-possesion that made you feel she never entirely gave herself even to her husband and children. Her sympathy for others was quick and warm, unless it was their own stubbornness or folly that was making them unhappy; then she seemed to withdraw for she had little sympathy with self-pity.

Neither our own qualities nor our Olympian friends could shield us from the blow that had fallen on us the previous winter. N'suto, my father, had been supervising the shifting of some trade goods in our warehouse. The rope holding a net full of amphorae broke and the heavy clay containers cascaded down on his head. One struck him on the temple. He lingered till my mother came, then died in her arms after a few whispered words. It was easy to overlook my father, for he was a quiet man, contented with his work and his family. But when he died it was as if the central pillar of the house had broken; our lives fell down about our ears.

When we came back to the house after the funeral, my mother gestured to me to follow her to her room. She sat in a low-backed chair and looked up into my face. She was a lovely woman still and somehow in that moment seemed younger and a stranger; she might have been the girl who had set sail for Kaphtu so many years ago. Her words were somehow not a surprise. "I'm leaving Karia, Akademus, my son. I don't know for how long. I'm going first to Attika where Dion and Ariadne are calling a thaisos for Dion's Dance. There's something in that Dance that I never needed before, but I think I need it now."

I was silent, for Dion's Dance was a women's mystery. I knew that most tales about it were foolish, though I knew nothing of what it really was. But I was happy to think that my mother would be with Ariadne.

She continued in a lower voice, "After that, I may visit my parents' graves and then...I don't know. While your father lived, I was happy with my life here. Now I feel restless. You children don't need me anymore..." I made some gesture and started to speak but she shook her head. "No, you don't. Your sister M'pha will take over the household and mother the young ones; it's just what she needs at this age. She'll have her chance for adventure when she grows up a bit. I'll see to that. And even without—this—you would have been going off adventuring soon, wouldn't you?"

For a moment I couldn't reply. Had my instinctive resistance to the thought of my mother leaving been based on love of her or on the fear that if she left I would be caught in a trap of responsibility for the household, for my father's trading ventures? My mother seemed to read my thoughts.

"Were you afraid I'd ask you to stay here and run things?" she asked gently. "You're too young to be trapped by that much responsibility. M'pha and your grandmother will see that the house and the trade are safe, and your uncle will have a chance to take charge of the overseas trade for awhile. Your grandmother and your aunt M'pha will keep him from doing anything foolish, don't worry about that. Where will you go Akademus, my son? To Kaphtu?"

I found my voice at last. "Yes, mother. I've always wanted to see Kaphtu. The great House at N'sos, the bulldance in the Great Court, the room of the Path..."

She smiled, a ghost of her old smile, but it was good to see her smile at all. "Britomartis filled your head with too many tales. I hope you're not disappointed. I hear Kaphtu has changed. Have your own adventures, my son. Don't try to relive ours. But you need to find your wings, as I need to regain mine. We'll see each other again, perhaps before we think possible now. And we have powerful protectors and messengers: our Olympian friends won't forget us. Just don't depend on them too much. They help those who help themselves and—some things—they can't help with at all." She bowed her head then, and I could see tears in her eyes. I went to her and took her awkwardly into my arms, comforting her as she had so often comforted me.

It was not that easy, of course; both my mother and I had to stand up to endless family arguments. My sister M'pha was torn between delight at the idea of running things at home and a longing to go adventuring with me. My uncle was secretly delighted to have the chance to be the titular head of the House of P'sero but felt he had to seem outraged at the idea of my mother going off alone and me, as he put it, "running away from my responsibilities."

But my grandmother, who was the only one in the family who might possibly have won an argument with my mother, was on our side, and I found to my surprise that I had a streak of my mother's ruthlessness in me too. The hardest thing for us both was leaving the younger children, but we both knew that half their protests were against the idea of being left in the charge of their older sister, which would do them no harm at all.

So eventually we both left on the same day, the first safe sailing day in spring, my mother in one of our best ships sailing directly to Phaleron on the Attilcan coast, and I as a passenger in a Syrian ship bound for Rhodes, where I would change ships for Kaphtu, since relations between Kaphtu and Karia had been bad for some years and a direct voyage was unwise. I knew as much about sea-trading as my father could teach me, which was a great deal, and, as it happened, I was able to ship from Rhodes to Kaphtu as supercargo on another Syrian trading ship. I was sitting beside the captain of that ship in the wineshop on the docks at Amnisos when a slender young man came in the door. I sat with my wine cup halfway to my lips while every bit of past experience clamored that this was an Olympian, as dangerous and unpredictable as the wildest of bulls.

Chapter Two
AKAMA

I managed to get my wine to my lips and drink it and I think the Olympian did not notice me then. He went quietly to a table near the door and sat down. The wineshop was so busy that unless you shouted for service you were not likely to be served, and he had a chance to observe the scene around him without being disturbed. It was a crowded and varied scene, well worth looking at, as I had already discovered. In the time of the former king (who was still called M'nos since Theseus did not use the title), both trade with Kaphtu and landing privileges at Amnisos had been tightly controlled. The wineshop was a concession to the few foreign vessels which landed and was run by palace servants. Sailors had to turn in their trade goods to a palace official, who gave them pieces of leaf or scraps of papyrus marked with special symbos, which they could then trade for wine. Now, I noticed sailors chaffered directly with the wineshop owner as they did in most ports.

Scraps of bronze, especially in the form of arrowheads, are the common trade goods for small trades, but I had already encountered some of the bits of bronze roughly stamped with a bull's head which Theseus was trying to introduce as common currency both in Kaphtu and in Attika. These "bulls" or "bulls' heads" seemed to be what most of the sailors traded for wine; even my Syrian captain had a few. As a trader, I liked the idea of a standard unit of trade for small goods, but after Theseus died the idea was soon forgotten and I think there are few of these little bull's-head tokens which have not been melted down for the bronze.

Theseus had made Amnisos a free port, as Phaleron had always been, and there were sailors from every oceangoing race in the wineshop and even a few traders from peoples like the Egyptians, who do not venture their own boats on the open sea. Another change since the time of M'nos was the presence of a great many Kaphtui in the wineshop. In the old days, Kaphtui had been kept out of the wineshop and foreigners had been confined to the dock area, so there was little contact between most Kaphtui and foreigners. This had its disadvantages, but one advantage was that it would have kept out a group like the noisy young Kaphtui aristocrats who were getting increasingly drunk at a table near the center of the room. I noticed with interest that although they all wore the kilts, the tightly clasped wide belts and the elaborately curled hair which men if their class would have worn in M'nos's time, about half of them were definitely Danaan in features and coloring. Theseus's long-distance rule of Kaphtu was having more impact than I had thought.

One of the noisiest of the aristocrats passed abruptly from conviviality to belligerence, as drunks will. Unfortunately, when he looked around for someone to pick a quarrel with he caught me looking at the group and that was enough to set him off. He got up and lurched toward me. I was dressed much as he was but was a stranger, and such a man would know most of his social equals at least by sight. So he

demanded loudly why some lice-eaten foreigner dared
to ape the appearance of a Kaphtui gentleman.

I sighed and reached for my dagger in its heavily
loaded sheath; one tap with that in the right place
would quiet him down without too much damage. I
only hoped I would not have to fight all of his friends
too. Unfortunately for my attacker, however, his
lurchings brought him up against the table where the
disguised Olympian sat. The drunken man, still
concentrating on me, shouted an insult and would have
passed on. But the Olympian rose to his feet and barred
the way. The drunken aristocrat tried to push past him,
and I suddenly felt an intense sympathy for him.

With good reason. I don't know if the Olympian
even touched him—he wouldn't have had to, of
course—but the drunken man, probably sobered by the
shock, staggered back as though a horse had kicked
him. He landed in a tangle of limbs on an empty table,
which collapsed under him, landing him on the floor
with an arm and a leg at odd angles. I was pretty sure
that some bones were broken; then, since everyone else
was standing gaping, I found myself taking charge, as I
would have at sea, or in my father's warehouse if an
accident had occurred.

I went over to the fallen man, giving the Olympian
a wide berth. "Get a Healer, quick," I snapped at one
of the waiters. "Stand back, you fools," I told the
suddenly sobered group at the table. "No one touch
him until the Healer gets here. This man has bones
broken."

One of the fallen man's drinking companions
turned pale and looked as if he were going to be sick.

"He can't have," the man mumbled foolishly. "He's a Leaper. He has to perform in the Dance soon."

My mother had inculcated in me some of her own feeling for the Dance, and I felt personally outraged. "Is this the way he keeps training? Just as well he won't Dance," I said angrily. "Who is he anyway?"

The man who had spoken before replied, "Rianisu, son of Riatano. He can't be hurt as badly as you say."

I looked at the injured man's features with sudden interest. His father had been a friend of my mother's in the days when she was a Dancer. In fact, this young man ws the grandson of Riadamantes. King of Karia. Riatano himself, I recalled, had been killed in a battle with Argive raiders. Whoever had had the bringing up of this young man had not, by the look of things, done much of a job. I said, half thinking aloud, "He's kin to friends of mine then. I'm glad he never finished picking his quarrel with me."

Several of the men at the table looked sharply at me and might have questioned me, but another man broke in. "What happened to him?"

From the crowd a voice came, sounding very positive. "Tried to push past a man at that table there, lost his balance and fell over his own feet." Everyone seemed to accept that, and I wondered if I had been the only one to see what had really happened. The table was empty now. It occurred to me later that the positive voice from the crowd might have been that of the Olympian himself.

A Healer bustled in, an old man in a robe with a torn hem. He seemed competent, and after listening to him clearing the crowd out of the way and getting the injured man carried out on a tabletop, I concluded that the torn robe was due to impatience rather than poverty; he had probably torn it off himself for a bandage in some emergency. Riatano's son seemed to be in good hands. I turned back to my table. Then I heard the man who had identified Rianisu saying to his companions, "*I'm* not going to tell the Mistress of the Dance. She'd have me skinned alive for being here with him. Who can we possibly get to replace him? The novices aren't ready and they let R'tosu sail to Athens..."

Suddenly a mad idea sprang full-blown into my head. With a brief excuse to the Syrian captain, I pushed my way out of the wineshop and climbed the steep streets of Anmisos until I found the paved road to N'sos. I followed it, feeling I was walking in one of Aunt Brit's stories. There were palace guards at some points along the road but they made no effort to stop me. If they had orders to stop anyone it was not one who looked as much like a prosperous Kaphtui as I did.

When I came to the great House, the palace of M'nos at N'sos, I tried not to gape. I was feeling it all the more now that I was alone, this landscape which had been part of the stories of my childhood. There had been a stab when we docked at Amnisos; my father had first seen my mother at that dock, when she came from Athens in his father's ship. But there had been too many people around for me to stand and dream. The wineshop, too, held a story; Britomartis had saved Theseus's life there when he was attacked by enemies from Athens. Now it held other memories for me: the deadly punishment of the drunken Rianisu for jostling the Olympian.

I was crossing the causeway now, past the guest house for distinguished visitors, and guards at the west gate looked at me curiously as I turned right and followed the path along the walls. I passed the south end of the House and made for a grove of trees that I hoped still marked the practice ground for the Dance. There was a guard at the entrance to the ground who looked as if he might stop me, so I spoke first. "Take me to the Mistress of the Dance," I said in my best imitation of my father's authoritative manner. It might not have worked in a smaller or better run palace. The guards at Riadamantes palace at home would have politely but firmly asked a stranger for his authority or business. But the palace of N'sos is immense and I had seen plenty of signs that discipline was slack.

The guard saluted and led the way into the ground. The bull was not being played and I saw no other Dancers, but near one end of the court I saw a slender girl in a Dancer's kilt conferring with a heavyset older man, who I guessed must be one of the handlers who took care of the bull outside of the Dance. I nodded a dismissal to the guard, and after a moments uncertainty he returned to his post.

I don't know what made me sure that this girl was the Mistress of the Dance, perhaps something in the guard's attitude as we came up to her. At first, she ignored me or perhaps didn't see me, deep as she was in conversation with the handler. The handler himself was immediately aware of me and kept darting glances at me. Eventually, without breaking off her discussion, the girl gave me a sidelong glance. This gave me my first shock, for she might have been Ariadne herself, or at least a younger sister of Ariadne. The hair so black it was blue in some lights, the little nose with the slight hook, the delicate arch of the eyebrows were all the same. The expression was the great difference. Ariadne was in love with Dion and deligted with her children;even setting aside the strength and joy which is the lot of the Immortals, she was a happy woman. This girl had a certain quality of sulkiness and petulance. It showed around her eyes and mouth. But she had strength; if she had been hurt she had fought back, too.

Initially, I had paid no attention to what the two were saying, but first a word and then a phrase caught my interest. The Dance, like any art or craft, has its technical terms, and in telling us stories my mother and Britomartis had used them without thinking and then had to explain them. I was pleased to find that I could follow the conversation without difficulty and even had some knowledge of the problems they were discussing. The girl was now definitely aware of me and was deliberately keeping me waiting. When they raised a topic I knew something about I thought it was time to make my presence felt.

"With permission, Bright Lady," I said, "most years the Dancers have worked barefoot; wearing boots on the Court of the Dance is the exception, not the rule. But it's up to the Mistress or Master of the Dance."

The girl faced me fully and gave me a smile that momentarily removed the petulance from her face.

"Bright Lady" she repeated. "I haven't been called that for awhile. Where are your lands, my lord, and what do you know of the Dance?"

Kaphtui is an old and subtle tongue and it is easy to pay a compliment or an insult in it by a delicate shift in language…I had called her "P'ne," "Bright Lady," which was a title appropriate for a goddess, a high priestess or a queen. A more usual form of address for a priestess or noblewoman was "P'dania", "Lady of the bright goddess." The Danaans have seized on this form of address, which they pronounce "Potnia" and which they use for any woman of consequence. But Kaphtui delight in ringing subtle changes on words: "P'ne" and "P'dania" and "P'dane," which means "bright lady-goddess" and which is properly applied only to a goddess; it is outrageous flattery when said to a mortal.

The words she had said to me were equally loaded with subtle implications. For "lord" she had used neither the Danaan form "kurios" nor the equivalent Kaphtu "koroiano," which means "man of the Great Lord." Instead she had used the Kaphtui "Koro," which means "Great Lord," and is the male equivalent of the term I had used to her. It could be used to a god, a high priest or a king. And in asking where I had come from she asked not for my "place," "so," but for my "place of rule," "sosu," implying that I was a ruler or at least one who had independent holdings under a High King. My use of the title to her had been automatic. It was a title I would have used for Aphea or Ariadne on a formal occasion. Her use of the similar term to me was ironic—not quite an insult but a rebuke for using forms too high-flown for the occasion.

All this passed through my mind in an instant, along with calculations as to how much it would be safe to tell her of myself. "I have just come from Rhodes, P'dania," I said, evading her first question and giving her the less exalted title. ìI know of the Dance because my mother was a Dancer. She and my father left Kephtu about the time of the Great Wave."

She smiled more gently and touched my arm in a quick impulsive gesture. "I am sorry for laughing at your good manners. A Dancer's child is welcome on this ground, and especially the child of a Dancer from the time before the Great Wave—cousin."

I wracked my mind to untangle the subtleties of that last word. Anyone who looked as much like Ariadne as this girl would have to be kin to the old kings of Kaphtu. But she must know as well as I that for the years just before the Great Wave the Dancers had been Athenians.

Suddenly I realized who this girl must be: the daughter of Theseus and Ph'dare. If Theseus had not changed the old customs, she was not only a princess but the future queen of Kaphtu; her husband would become the next M'nos. She would have been called Ariadne in the old days, for that is a title as well as a personal name, but Theseus had never taken the title of M'nos; she too might have kept her birth-name. I gave some information, hoping to get some.

"My mother's name is Alceme, my father was N'suto, son of P'sero. If we are cousins, lady, we are very distant ones."

The handler, whom we had both forgotten, gave a soft exclamation. The girl nodded permission to speak,

and he burst out eagerly. "My Lord, I saw your mother
Dance when I was a child. Phane, they called her, the
Golden Lady. She was one of the Dancers when the
Lady Kariase was Mistress of the Dance. But this
young lord takes after his father's side, my lady. His
face is the face of your grandfather, M'nos the Dark." I
looked at the man sharply. He was short and round-
headed, one of Old People like my grandmother
Riamare. It was supposed to be a closely guarded
family secret that my father was M'nos and not P'sero,
but I wondered if my grandmother had deceived
herself about the secrecy of her premarital affair with
M'nos. If only the Old People knew the secret was safe
enough; they were as close-mouthed as they were
stubborn.

The girl, at any rate, showed no signs of
recognizing the double meaning of the handler's "takes
after his father." She smiled again and said, "I think I
will claim you as a cousin. The Athenian Dancers then
were all kin to my grandfather Aegeus, just as the
Kaphtui Dancers are all kin to the House of M'nos.
You may call me Akama. No one calls me Ariadne in
private. What is your name, cousin?"

I smiled back. This girl, I thought, could easily be a
hellion if she turned against you but for the moment I
had caught her fancy. "My birth-name is Akademus,
lady, but my friends are in the habit of calling me
Ducalion." That was another half-truth. My Danaan
friends do call me Ducalion, but it is a corruption of
my Kaphtui nickname, Dukariano, which means "lion
of Karia," or if you want to be uncomplimentary, "the
beast of Karia," a nickname that survives from my

wild youth when I was trying to prove myself and making a lot of trouble for others in the process.

Akama looked at me very seriously. "I wish you well, Ducalion," she said softly.

I felt something important was happening as I looked into the dark eyes and said solemnly, "And I wish you well, Akama." It seemed as good a time as any to break my news, and I went on. "But I fear I bring bad tidings. A young man named Rianisu was injured in an accident in Amnisos. I think some bones are broken. I understand that he's one of your Leapers."

Her eyes lit up with wrath I was glad was not directed at me. "Where?" she rapped out sternly.

"In the wineshop on the docks," I said after a moment's hesitation.

She nodded grimly and turned to the handler. "Broken bones or not, I won't have him back, S'tono. He's been warned away from the wineshop before. He's had his last chance, whatever they say."

I wondered who "they" were, as the handler, S'tono, said in reply, "All very well, my lady, but who can take his place? This year's novices are far from ready and too many of the Trainers have been allowed to leave their duties. You'd never get R'tosu back in time…"

She shook her head. "I don't want R'tosu. If last year's Dancers had done their jobs the novices would be ready. Surely a novice can be found to do a Roll Under. Even if we make a poor show at the first Dance, we'll have four Leapers and be within the Laws."

S'tono shook his head gloomily and started to speak, but I cut in.

"Akama—my lady—I came not just to bear news but to offer a suggestion. There is no Dance outside Kaphtu, but my mother trained me in all the moves, and I've even had a little practice with a bull. The Mistress of the Dance has great power in emergencies; she can do practically anything to make sure the Dance is fitly performed. Take me in the injured man's place. I won't fail you." I held my breath as Akama looked into my eyes again. This was the wild idea that had sent me hurrying to N'sos. If it succeeded, I would not only be reliving the adventures of my mother and her friends, I would be in close contact with this girl for the remainder of the year, and that was already very important for me.

Her eyes seemed to bore into mine as she said softly, almost to herself, "I'd like to...they'd all say...but what else...I'll do it! At least I'll give you the chance. S'tono, go let out the bull." He made a gesture of protest and she repeated in a voice that left no room for argument, "Let out the bull." He turned and went toward the stockade at the end of the practice court. Without saying another word, Akama went to the end of the practice field opposite the stockade and stood waiting. I quickly unlaced my boots. Even if I hadn't preferred to jump barefoot, I would have needed special soft-soled boots for leaping the bull. I cinched my belt a little tighter and ran my hands through my hair, then set myself for a side leap.

The holder whistled to tell us he was ready, and Akama raised her arm in a gesture that I recognized: it meant "send me the bull." In a moment, heavy doors creaked and the bull trotted out onto the field, snorting and pawing. He looked at me and pawed the ground, then Akama gave a shrill whistle to attract his attention. The massive head swung toward her and the bull started a trot toward her that changed into a charge. I did a simple side leap; a run to the bull, a jump and a handstand on his back, landing on my feet on the other side of the path. His attention was on Akama and he hardly changed stride as I went over. If you judge the bull's speed right, the side leap is not all that hard. I've done it on a horse, which is both taller and faster than a bull. Also, by the time you reach the bullís back, his head, which is the most dangerous part of him, has gone by.

I looked toward the top of the field in time to see Akama do her head leap. Running to meet the bull, she grasped the horns and let the bull's toss throw her over his head, her back arching as she went until her feet touched the bull's back; then she let go of the horns and let her momentum carry her forward to do a handspring on the bull's rump and so to the ground, landing on her feet. Her control of her own body was good, but I didn't like the sideways roll of his head as she released the horns or the speed with which the bull turned and followed Akama as she ran diagonally over to near my former position. The bull is supposed to turn, but he is supposed to run back straight down the court, not, as this one did, almost pursue the Leaper. She got him back on track in time for us to make our simultaneous side leaps that took us over the bull at the same time, so that for an instant our hurtling bodies were perfectly in line, perpendicular to the bull's back. But there was a toss of the bull's head that shouldn't have happened. It brought the great horns dangerously close to my side as I went over.

Akama let the bull continue his run back to the stockade. I could tell from her smile and shining eyes that I had passed my test. But there was a cold feeling at the pit of of my stomach. For all her grace and daring, this girl, who was supposed to be the Tauromath of her Dancers, was not in proper control of her bull. And if I became one of her Leapers, I might very well be signing my own death warrant.

Chapter Three
THE SEAL STONE

She must have seen it in my face; the light went out of her eyes like a lamp blown out. I admired her tremendously as she said in a voice that was almost as indifferent as she tried to make it, "You pass the test, but do I? Will you be one of my Leapers, Ducalion?"

There was suddenly no question in my mind, and I took her hands in mine and touched my forehead to the backs of her hands. "I am your man, lady," I said formally.

She bit her lip and tears came to her eyes. "Even though I can't control my bull?" she asked with a catch she couldn't quite keep out of her voice.

"Even so, lady," I told her looking into her eyes. "But you can control him, otherwise you'd never have turned him. You have the Tauromath power; you just don't have it under control. Have you walked the Path to find your own symbol for your amulet?"

She shook her head and dashed the tears from her eyes, "My father utterly forbids me to set foot on the Path. He said if I couldn't be Tauromath without it, I should give up being Tauromath. I tried to prove that I could do it, but it's always like this. I strain every nerve and just barely keep the bull under control. It hangs on a thread." She gave me a wry smile. "This was one of my better days. In the Great Court, with the crowds…"

I nodded somber agreement. Even a bull well under control on the practice court could act up on his first real Dance. I tried to think of something helpful. "Have you tried every amulet you can get your hands on? Even with amulets not made for you, some are more attuned to you than others."

She gave me a startled glance. "No," she said slowly. "I use one my mother gave me. I had no idea it could make a real difference. One of my ladies is a priestess. I'll send her to gather every old seal stone she can find. But how will I know the right one? Can you tell me?"

I shook my head. "I have no Power at all," I told her, "but I'm told on good authority that the right one should feel warm in your hand." I suddenly had an idea. "Try to find one that belonged to your aunt: your mother's sister Ariadne, I mean. You look like her; your minds may be alike too." That was an indiscretion but she didn't think to ask me how I knew what Ariadne looked like. She had probably been told of the resemblance before by others.

Her eyes lit up. "There's an old chest in my room that belonged to her. I'll look there first. S'tono, take him to the Dancer's quarters and get him fitted out. Ducalion, tell them you're taking Rianisu's place by my orders and tell them if they want to argue to argue with me. Don't stand for any nonsense from them. I'll come to the Common Room when I've checked the chest." She started toward the palace, then turned and smiled shyly. "Thank you, Ducalion. Even if it doesn't work, thank you." Then she was gone.

S'tono smiled at me a little ruefully. "That's the way she is, my lord, quick off the mark and won't be denied. She has a great heart, greater than her strength sometimes. She needs true friends."

I looked into his dark eyes. "I think she has one in you, S'tono. But then you're one of the True People, aren't you, one of the Children of Kariatu?" I used the old names I had learned from my grandmother but he didn't look surprised. I suspected he knew very well who N'suto's mother had been.

He looked at me without expression and said, "Yes, my lord, and we don't forget. But my lady needs better friends than an old bull handler. Will you follow me, my lord, to the Dancer's quarters?"

Of course it was all vey well for her to tell me to take no nonsense from the other Dancers, but quite naturally there was a tremendous uproar. Dancers train together as novices for a year. By the time they are ready for their first Dance they are a close-knit group and will react strongly to an attempt to introduce a stranger into their ranks. I stonewalled as politely as I could while their indignation got hotter and louder. The fact that I had been in the wineshop when Rianisu was hurt was soon given a sinister interpretation: no one quite accused me of nobbling him to get his place in the Dance but they soon would have.

Akama heard enough before she came into the room to put her into a towering rage. As she strode into the Common Room she almost gave out sparks. The chorus of angry voices came to a ragged halt and she spoke to complete silence in a low, soft voice that somehow made my blood run cold.

"Rianisu is a popinjay who injured himself by his own folly. Not a single novice or Trainer is ready to take his place. The Lord Ducalion comes to us as a gift from the gods. His mother was a great Dancer and the two leaps he did with me made all of you look like children playing at the Dance. He is going to save us all from being laughing-stocks at our first Dance. An insult to him is an insult to me. Any more of your foolishness and I'll send you all to your homes and replace you with the novices. The difference would hardly be noticeable." By the time she was through they were looking like a group of scolded children. She turned on her heel and said over her shoulder, "Lord Ducalion, join me at your leisure in the Great Court. I have something to show you." She went out, leaving us all shaken, including me. It was not just her royal power either, it was sheer force of personality.

The young man whom I managed to identify in the hubbub as the remaining male Leaper turned toward me with an apologetic smile. "The old people say that when she's in a rage she's like her grandfather, the Dark M'nos. Forgive our foolishness, my lord…"

I interrupted him. "Just Ducalion, please. We're going to be partners in the Dance, let's try to be friends too." The Leaper grinned and clasped my hand.

A slender, sallow girl who had said little so far came up and said with a sniff, "You'll have no more trouble with *them* from now on. And what business is it of the Ground Dancers anyhow, if the Leapers are satisfied? She must, then, be the other female Leaper. She offered her hand and I took it. Like many female leapers, she was boyish both in figure and in manner. She smiled a little sourly. "Better not keep her waiting for all her 'at your leisure,'" she said. I nodded, smiled at the others and followed her out of the room. I would have to learn all their names as soon as I could.

After a few hesitations and one false turn, I found my way to the Great Court without having to ask. The bustling scene in the Great Court was subdued for once. Akama was pacing up and down on one side of the court and there was a wide empty lane created by people keeping well out of her way. The usual idlers and loungers in the court whom Akama had probably impatiently ordered to carry on as usual were giving a sort of self-conscious imitation of their usual gossip and bustle. That one small dark-haired girl in a temper could have such an effect on a lively Kaphtui crowd was a demonstration of her force of character. The thought crossed my mind that this was one of the few mortal women I had met who could stand up to my mother and grandmother. It was lucky for me that I was used to living with strong-willed women.

I smiled at her when she saw me and almost reluctantly she smiled back. The buzz and bustle in the court became a little more natural as she let go of her rage. "Have you ever tried getting angry at the bull?" I asked.

She looked startled. "It's not the bull's fault if he resists me," she said. "It's his nature. I never get angry at animals. But those fools in there…!" She was getting angry again and I tried to get her back to the subject.

"Nevertheless," I said, "the same will that cowed that group of Dancers can control a bull. All you need to do is focus it."

She laughed at me, not entirely believing me. "The bull doesn't know I'm the king's daughter," she said with a short laugh. "Nor does he care."

I shook my head. "They weren't afraid of the king, they were afraid of your anger." I left that to sink in and asked, "What did you want to show me?"

Her face lit up. "Come in here," she said, pulling me into a nearby doorway. "No one ever comes in her now and we'll be private." There was a guard at the door who looked uneasy as we went in but she ignored him as if he had been invisible.

As my eyes grew used to the dim light I realized where we were—a smallish room with a rectangular pit in the center of the floor divided from another room a few steps up by a low wall with three pillars. In the higher room I could see a stone chair flanked by wall paintings of earless gryphons. Even Akama was subdued when she looked at the stone chair. "The throne of my fathers," she murmured. "You know where we are?"

My own voice was subdued as I said, "Yes, the Room of the Path. You're not thinking of…"

She looked at me in surprise. "Of course not. To go down the Path you need priestesses, a chant, the whole ceremony. I came here because it's not used now, as I said." I said nothing. I knew that in certain circumstances the Path could be walked with no preparation at all. And whether anyone walked the Path or not, it was still a place where the three worlds came very close together. I had learned enough from Aunt Brit to know that. Since Theseus was the son of Posudi, this girl had a Great Olympian for a grandfather. She had at least Seven Powers, her power over animals. I wondered if this point of strain between worlds had a fascination for her that she was unaware of.

But she had dismissed our surroundings from her mind and was eagerly pulling something out of her belt: a small seal stone. "I found this in the chest I told you about. It makes my whole hand and arm feel warm, my old seal is nothing in comparison to it. Do you feel anything when you touch it?"

I looked at the little carved seal and touched it with my hand. It bore the figure of a goddess holding a small tree. "No," I murmured abstractedly. "I told you I don't have the Power." But something about that seal was naggingly familiar. Something in a story of Aunt Brit's. Not her own seal; that was the gryphon killing a flying serpent. Who's seal, then, would she have described to me? Ariadne's! Yes, I remembered the story now. But a seal was a very personal thing. Would Ariadne have left it here when she fled with Theseus? Had I ever seen Ariadne wearing a seal? For a moment I could almost see this seal on a fine chain around her wrist and then doubt struck me. Was my imagination playing tricks? If Ariadne had taken her seal to the Bright Land how could it have found it's way into a chest in N'sos?

Then I realized that in one sense it didn't matter. Amulets and chants and ceremonies were all merely ways of focusing the mind. The Olympians themselves had no need of such aids. If Ariadne had kept her seal it was for sentimental reasons, not to use it as a tool.

I looked Akama in the eyes and spoke with as much force as I could, "There's a good chance that this is Ariadne's seal. If it is, I think it may help you a great deal. She was a great Tauromath and a great Leaper. Try to think of her when you use the seal."

She gave me a strange look. "Ariadne is dead, isn't she?" she asked, oddly hesitant.

I temporized. "Is that what you've been told?" I asked cautiously. There were secrets involved that could cause trouble if too lightly revealed.

She looked away from me toward the door and put a hand on my arm. "That's what my father says, but he won't say how or anything except that it happened on Naxos after they all left Kaphtu. My mother won't talk about it at all. And Uncle Menesthius just tells me to ask my parents. Ariadne was the eldest, the heiress. I've sometimes wondered if...It's a terrible thing to think about one's own parents but..."

I took both her hands in mine without thinking, and looked into her eyes. "Akama, there are some secrets involved that aren't mine to tell, but I assure you you're wrong about your mother and father. Ariadne is no longer in this world, but she left Theseus of her own free will and told him to marry Ph'dare and take the throne with her blessing. I know Ariadne would wish you well and want to help you if she were here."

Akama looked at me with an intent expression. I suddenly realized that was an acute and devious intelligence behind that lovely face. She and I, had common ancestors a few generations back. I had the family face, it seemed, but she perhaps had some of the power to question and plan that had kept the House of M'nos on the throne of Kaphtu for so many years. I thought again that this was the first woman I had met that did not pale into insignificance beside my mother and her Olympian friends. "Out of this world," she repeated. "out of this world"—not 'dead.' The same words my father used. I won't press you now but I want to know more about that. And you said 'Ariadne left Theseus.' Does that mean my father wanted her first, not my mother? No, you don't need to answer. I can see it in your face. No wonder my mother hates her sister so much, if she was my father's second choice."

I had heard the story from Ariadne's point of view and I had had some sympathy with Theseus, who had courted both sisters in pursuit of an alliance between Athens and Kaphtu, and had been left with Ph'dare by Ariadne's choice, not his own. It occurred to me now how that whole business must have rankled with Ph'dare. It would certainly not help much to tell Akama that her father had courted both sisters simultaneously. Indeed, unless and until I decided to tell Akama the whole story. I had better say as little as possible. Her shrewdness had half-guessed the truth from the little I had said already.

"My lady," I said more formally, letting go of her hands a little awkwardly, "I hope I will be free someday to tell you all I know. I thank you for not asking me more now." I would have to use my trader's skill as a shield against her intelligence. She had said that she wouldn't ask me about one thing, not that she wouldn't ask any more questions. But a trader is quick to put more meaning into a buyer's words than are in them, as when you say "I am glad my lady likes the merchandise. Will you take all or just a part?" I don't suppose I fooled this shrewd young princess really, but she was content to let it drop for the moment.

"How can I test the amulet?" she asked next. I considered quickly. Power to control animals is the same Power as power to control humans. There was some barrier in this girl's mind to control of the bull, but she was used to imposing her will on humans. "If the amulet is as good as I think," I told her, "you can control people with it, not just animals. Concentrate on the guard outside the door. Make him come in and hand his spear to me. It will be a good test of your control because a soldier hates to give up his weapons to a stranger."

She looked at me unbelievingly and then took the seal stone in her hand and looked toward the door. For a moment nothing happened, then the guard stepped inside. I looked into his eyes and suppressed a shudder; he was well under control, aware of nothing. I don't like to see a human being under control. I knew that my Olympian friends didn't either and used the power only when unavoidable. I wished I could have thought of a different way to strengthen Akama's confidence in her powers, but this opportunity was too good to miss.

The guard, of course, was used to taking orders and would have obeyed a verbal order to do what he was doing now. There was a little hesitation in handing his spear to me, but no more than he might have shown if he had been in possession of his own mind and had been given a verbal order to do it. I spoke to Akama, partly to show her that she could control the guard without total concentration. "Lady, never misuse this power." I touched the spear to the man's chest. "I could kill this poor fellow without his being able to do a thing about it. Have him take his spear back and return to his post. Question him if you like as we go out; he'll remember nothing." The guard's hand closed on the spear and he walked out and took up his post. Akama opened her hand and looked at the little seal stone unbelievingly.

"I felt his hand open and close," she said in an awed voice. "It was as if I were doing it. I felt his body move as if it were mine but I couldn't feel his thoughts..."

I shook my head. "He had no thoughts while you controlled him. From what I've been told, you should feel the bull's movements as you did the guard's. A good Tauromath controls the bull from inside, so to speak, or so I've been told."

She nodded. "I think I can do it now," she said almost to herself. "Before, I was always pushing from the outside, moving the bull like a dead weight. But he's alive. I've got to live in him somehow, move his muscles as I do my own." She looked at me with wide eyes. "Ducalion, I'm frightened."

I nodded somberly. "Power is frightening. The Seven Powers especially, because they aren't natural to mortals. But any power carries responsibility and responsibility is frightening—captaining a ship, being in charge of a trade venture, running a household. Only a fool thinks power is just something to enjoy. You know this; you're a princess."

She shook her head and looked at me with pain-shadowed eyes. "No, Ducalion. I know very little of power. I've never had much. I've been my father's pawn, and my mother's. Right now factions here in Kaphtu are trying to use me for their own purposes. So long as I was powerless I was no threat to them. But now, with your help, I'm getting some power. They won't like that. Perhaps we're no longer in danger from the bull, but we're still very much in danger. Do you love danger, Ducalion, as my father does?"

I shook my head. "I'm a merchant, not an adventurer, my lady. I'll face danger if I have to, but I'll keep out of it if I can. And I'll keep you out of it too, if I'm able to."

She shook her head and gave me her lovely smile, tinged with sadness. "You won't be able to," she said.

Chapter Four
THE THREAT

Looking back, I can see that we were too incautious about letting others see Akama's new power over the bull She was soon so much in control that she could easily have made it look as if she were still having trouble with the bull, but she was naturally eager to show off her new powers and I was still overconfident. It did not occur to me that the daughter of Theseus, the Ariadne of Kaphtu, could be in serious danger in her own palace. At first she may not have been. Knowing nothing of her new seal stone, her enemies probably thought at first that I was a Tauromath myself and had simply taken over control of the bull while pretending that Akama was controlling it. Whether they thought this or not, they knew that the unwelcome change in Akama followed closely on my arrival, so not surprisingly their first attack was on me.

For the first day or two I forgot all about my gear aboard the ship in Amnisos. But then the lack of a few small personal items reminded me that the ship would not stay in port forever and if I wanted my gear I had better get it. Besides, I owed the Syrian captain who had taken me on as supercargo thanks and a farewell. So after early practice on the third day since my arrival I made my way down to Amnisos. I was pleased with the progress I was making with the other Dancers, delighted with Akama's new confidence and fairly well satisfied with my progress as a Leaper. By my mother's standards I was not much of a Leaper, but my mother's standards were high and I showed to advantage in my present company.

I had forgotten that others besides the Dancers might resent my replacing Rianisu. The little knot of Kaphtui aristocrats who barred my way in a quiet street in Amnisos as I was on my way to the ship was mostly composed of the men who had been drinking wih Rianisu, but their ranks had been swelled by others. There were too many to fight and I did not want to run if I could help it. I would forfeit any respect they had for me if I did. If I could not talk my way out of a fight, I would have to try to taunt them into fighting me one at a time. If they were merely playboys I might survive. If they were real warriors I would not, but at least I had some chance against a series of single opponents; I would have none against a mob.

I stopped close to them but not too close and waited. If your opponent makes the first move he may make a mistake. There are occasions when it is best to be the first to act but they are rare. I tried to look as impassive as I could; not showing the expected reaction, or any reaction is often a good move. It was encouraging that the first of them to find voice was someone in the back row, not one of those standing face-to-face with me.

"Here he is," the voice said, "the foreign rat who snuck up to the palace and took an injured man's place."

I looked over the group before me and tried to speak in a friendly tone, even with a trace of humor. "Do you covet that place, then? Which of you can leap the bull?" If I could get them arguing with me on that level so much the better.

The same voice came again from the rear. "You're not fit to take Rianisu's place."

I looked at the man immediately in front of me. "Why not?" I asked. "Perhaps you can tell me since your friend in the rear seems to shy to look me in the face."

The man I addressed looked ill at ease. Despite being more or less in the center of the front row he was not, I thought, the leader of the group. But he answered, a little reluctantly, "He is the rightful king of Crete." I looked at him more closely; despite his Kaphtui appearance he must be a Danaan. He went on, "M'nos left no sons, so Rianisu as his brother's son should inherit the throne."

It was a victory to have gotten one of them to argue, and I pressed the advantage. "That is Danaan law, but this is Kaphtu. If Theseus is not the rightful ruler then Danaan law has no force in Kaphtu. But if he is, then Rianisu can't be." Lykos, who had taught me to ague, would have been proud of me for producing that on the spur of the moment. It was good enough to draw another one of them into the argument.

This one was definitely Kaphtui and he said, with a glare at the other man that was another victory for me, "It's not a question of Danaan law or Kaphtui law. Everyone knows what P'sephea was. Mínos left *no* of his own blood. But Rianisu is a true descendant of the House of M'nos."

I looked at him and said quietly, "The last I heard Riadamantes still lived and ruled in Karia."

There was an angry silence. They knew as well that Kaphtui hotheads who objected to Theseus's rule had contacted Riadamantes, who would have nothing to do with their plots. News of the offer had come to Theseus's ears and he had not believed in the sincerity of Riadamantes's refusal. Riadamantes was a man whose hot temper was usually under control, but he did not like having his word doubted, and the tone of Theseus's messages was insulting. Relations between Karia and Kaphtu had rapidly worsened, hence my circuitous route to Kaphtu and my reluctance to proclaim my homeland. These men evidently disliked Theseus's rule. Would it help to tell them that I was from Karia?

The silence was broken by a hard-faced man who stood next to the man Ihad questioned. "Enough of this! We are not here to debate with this man." He fixed his eyes on me with what he meant to be an intimidating stare. "It does not suit us for you to take Rianisu's place. Let the daughter of Theseus make a fool of herself at her first Dance." Angry men often say more than they mean to. I now knew the real reason for this confrontation. If Akama's first Dance was a success she would be a popular heroine; Kaphtui idolize a good Leaper. More popularity for Akama would spoil their plans to put Rianisu on the throne. Even though she now had a better amulet, the loss of me would at least shake her confidence and make her Dance a much less impressive one, with some poorly prepared novice thrust into my place. How far would they go to keep me out of the Dance?

I was not left in doubt long. The hard-faced man went on, "You have two choices. Get back on your ship and leave Kaphtu forever, or we'll break your arm and leg as Rianisu's is broken."

My temper rose, but I kept it in control; cold anger is a better weapon than hot. But I let enough anger show in my voice to let them feel it. "So you say. But I will not leave Kaphtu. You can't harm me by yourself, of course." I sneered at the hard-faced man, hoping to set him up for an individual fight. I might not win that fight—he looked like a warrior—but it was better than having them all rush me. I swept the crowd with my eyes.

"If you attack me in a pack like mongrel curs, you had better kill me. If I live I will hunt you down and kill you one by one. But if you kill me, better leave Kaphtu. Someone will talk, and the Princess Akama will hear of my death. I would not like to be any of you when she hears of it. And if you do not fear the vengeance of mortals, fear that of the immortal gods. The person of a Dancer is sacred. Strike at the Dance and you offend Posudi. The Shaker of the Earth is not lightly mocked.

I sometimes wonder if my words alone would have swayed them. I think I would have had to fight the hard-faced man, and if I had won that fight I might have gotten free of the rest of them. But as I finished speaking, their faces changed. They were looking not at me but behind me and there was a look of indescribable horror on their faces. Someone gave a sort of half-groan, half-sob and suddenly the whole group turned and ran as if pursued by demons.

I whirled around, my hand going to my belt knife, even though I knew that nothing against which a knife would be of any use would have brought that look of horror to their faces. When I saw what stood behind me, my hand left the knife and went to my brow in automatic salute. It was the figure of a young man, his face composed and his body relaxed, but no less deadly dangerous for that. He wore the same face he had worn in the wineshop, was almost certainly not real. But even without the same face I think I would have known him: the Olympian who had caused Rianisu's injuries in the wineshop. I wondered what my attackers had seen.

The Olympian spoke, and his voice seemed as ordinary as his face and form. "It seemed unfair that you should suffer for what happened in the wineshop," he said, his lips twitching into a brief half-smile.

"My thanks, Bright Lord," I said as calmly as I could. "That's two fights you've saved me."

His eyes drilled into mine. "How do you know who I am?" he asked softly, almost casually.

I was not deceived; he did not like having his disguise pierced. I answered cautiously, "My family has been honored with the friendship of some of those from the Bright Land."

His voice was still quiet, but the question came instantly. "Which ones?"

I looked into his face and answered in a tone tried to make match his own. "The Lady Britomartis, the Lady Ariadne and the Lord Dionysus."

His eyes flashed. "The half-mortals! That is no recommendation to my friendship, I assure you."

My brain raced. This was not, I was sure, either Zeus or Posudi. Not Hephaestus or Hermes either; they were friends and allies of my Olympian friends. That left Ares, spoiled and arrogant, and Apollo who I knew was unfriendly to my friends. I hoped it wasn't Ares. But wait, I had called him "P'ro," "Bright Lord." And "Aporo," holy bright Lord" was the Kaphtui version of "Apollo." And he had asked "How did you know me?" I decided to chance offending him by a wrong guess.

"If you are indeed the Son of Leto, my Lord, I have no wish to have you for an enemy. But I did not ask for your friendship." It was a bold speech to make to an Olympian but my gamble paid off: he chose to be amused rather than offended.

"No, mortal; it was, you might say, thrust on you. But I like your wit, and your courage. If I offer my friendship, will you take it?"

There was only one answer to that. "Most joyfully, Lord Apollo."

He nodded. "Good. I will make a claim on that friendship some day. I can see…"

His eyes went curiously blank and I remembered with a cold feeling at the back of my head that the Son of Leto had the rarest of the Seven Powers, the power of prophecy. My curiosity got the better of me. "Do you really see the future, my lord?"

He shook his head impatiently. "There's not just one future, but myriad possibilities, always shifting. some things become fixed, or nearly fixed as the possibilities shift and change. I see the changing possibilities, I see them grow stronger and weaker. And I see the shadows of those things which become

45

fixed amid the flux. But so do you, a little, my young friend of Olympíans."

I looked at him in astonishment. "But I have no Powers: I never have had." It was what I had always believed.

He smiled and shook his head. "You wouldn't recognize it. Nor, probably, would the three Olympians who know you. But haven't you always been 'lucky' in your guesses as to what would happen?"

I was silent. It was true enough; I had learned to trust my hunches and premonitions. Sometimes in a fight or a bargaining session I seemed to know the other person's move before he made it. But I had never thought of myself before as having any Power.

The seemingly ordinary young man before me went on. "I know my own. Athena and Britomartis see what truly is; I see what will or may be. Neither is always a comfortable Power to have. And I know that in some way before too long you will help me and I will help you. But I do not know your name." He finished with a smile.

"Akademus, lord," I said, my head in a whirl. "Son of Alceme and N'suto."

His eyes took on that blank look for a moment. "Alceme," he murmured. "She, too, is in the pattern but I can't see yet…" He looked at me, his eyes aware of me again. "For now, go on with what you have begun. Tell no lies to anyone, but tell the whole truth only to those who love you. You need have no fear of that rabble I chased away; seeing you will remind them of—unpleasant things. But they are only tools. Beware of those who mean to use those tools. Farewell for now."

Suddenly he was not there—something you have to get used to if you deal with Olympians. Was he standing now on this very hill in the Bright Land, a hill empty of houses and overlooking an empty harbor? Or had he gone elsewhere, perhaps directly to the Threshold of the the City of the Olympians? No mortal could know. The light of the Bright Land, which is power and delight to the Immortals, is death to us.

I went down to the harbor to say my farewells and get my gear from the ship with my mind racing. Sober, Rianisu might be more impressive than he had been drunk, but he did not strike me as the stuff of which leaders are made. So, likely, he was a pawn in the hands of some person or group who wanted to put him on the throne and rule through him. Not, I thought, the hard-faced man. I would guess that he was a capable and ruthless lieutenant, a follower of orders not a planner. So those who wanted Rianisu on the throne were still faceless, unless I could guess something about their messenger that could give me a clue. There had been something about the hard-faced man which had bothered me at the time: a trace of accent. He didn't speak quite like an Athenian or like an Attikan at all, though he was certainly not a Danaan, despite his Kaphtui dress. Where had I heard that accent?

Suddenly a memory came to my mind. An arrogant little group of emissaries from the High King at Mykenae who had called on Riadamantes to try to frighten him away from certain trade routes which the Argives were trying to take over. Kaphtui trade had suffered a good deal since the Great Wave. Not only had ships and ports been damaged but Theseus was an adventurer at heart, without the canny traders' instinct of the House of M'nos. He had not made the moves that he should have to reestablish trade, and newer nations were pushing into the space left by faltering Kaphtui trade. Karia and the Argives were rivals for this trade and the Argives wanted no rivals. The emissaries had gotten no satisfaction from Riadamantes and had soon left Karia, with none to regret their going. But their bearing and accent had stuck in my mind; and hard-face reminded me of them.

On my return to N'sos I requested and received a private interview with Akama. She received me in her own room, with a few of her ladies chattering together at the other end of the room for the sake of propriety, but well out of earshot. "My lady," I said formally, "I have some things to tell you that you may not like. Would you do me the favor of letting me tell the whole story before you question me or interrupt me?" Before she lost her temper was what I meant, and she probably realized this, for she smiled and settled herself in a chair before nodding for me to speak.

"To begin with, my lady, although I did just come from Rhodes, as I told you, my home is in Karia. I came here not for any political purpose but because of the stories my mother and others have told me about the Dance. Now I've been drawn into the politics of Kaphtu by taking Rianisu's place and by—what followed. Your enemies want to put Rianisu on the throne, I think, as their pawn. Despite your father's suspicions, Riadamantes had no ambitions for the throne of Kaphtu. I don't want you taken by surprise by the information that I'm from Karia. I'm pretty sure that your real enemies are neither Karians nor Kaphtui but Argives, probably agents of the High King at Mykenae. I don't know if they really hope to work through Rianisu as a puppet ruler or whether they just want to weaken Kaphtu for another military attack. I doubt if the young hotheads they're using know who's behind them."

I went on to tell her what happened on the road in Amnisos. Her eyes flashed but she held her tongue till I had finished. I said simply that they had threatened me and left, without saying why they had left. Things were complicated enough without bringing in the Olympian.

When I had finished, she took a deep breath and held in her temper with a visible effort. "Some of what told me I'd guessed already, but your information helps confirm my guesses. The trouble is, there's very little I can do. Oh, I can protect you from any direct attacks, but I can't do anything really effective about the rebels. I'm supposed to be my father's representative here, but I don't have any real powers. In fact, my father is so afraid of a viceroy getting too much power that he has the power here divided up between several men: one fo civil affairs, one for military, another one for trade. As a result, no one can act effectively. Uncle Menesthius might if he were here, because he's so respected and because my father trusts him. But Father is always calling him back to Athens, and no one else would act against people as highly placed as Rianisu's friends."

Then she looked at me and smiled a curious smile. She sent her ladies out of the room with a gesture. They looked scandalized but went. "I knew you were from Karia," she said. "S'tono knew that your grandparents had emigrated there. But I'm glad you told me. There are other things you haven't told me, I know, but I'll trust you to tell them to me in time."

"You can trust me, Akama," I said earnestly. "I've left out things but I've never lied to you and I never will."

She smiled that curious smile again. "I know, Ducalion," she said gently. "That's the other power I have, and it's stronger than my power over animals. I always know when anyone tries to lie to me."

Chapter Five
THE VALLEY

It was a surprise, of course, but since I had mo intention of ever lying to this girl, in one way it made no difference. The power to detect lies was, I supposed, a variant of the power of true sight, which Britomartis shared with Athena, her aunt. I would not have thought of lying to Aunt Brit either. But there was still a great deal I had not told this girl and it was important to me to know how much of that she knew or had guessed. "What else do you know about me that I haven't told you?" I asked bluntly.

Her eyes fell and then she looked into my face again and spoke a little hesitantly.

"You may not like my knowing this, Ducalion, but S'tono is devoted to me; he'll tell me secrets that he wouldn't reveal to anyone else. He says the Old People say that your father's father was the Dark M'nos."

I nodded, and I wondered if she was thinking what I was thinking, that in a curious way my descent from M'nos put me on a sort of equal basis with her, made the thoughts I was thinking about her not entirely ridiculous.

"It's not important," I said.

She smiled a curious smile. "Oh, it's important, all right. It's just not as important as other things."

I had meant that it wasn't important that she know of my ancestry. She had taken my words another way. My ancestry was important—for what? Not as important as what other things? I knew what I hoped she meant, but it seemed too soon for that. She went on without explaining those words. "There's something else too, Ducalion. Do you know what the Old People mean by the Daughter of Kariatu?"

I nodded. "It's the old line of rulers from when women ruled Kaphtu. All the women of the Old People call themselves daughters of Kariatu: the nymph of the island. But *the* Daughter of Kariatu is the woman who would be ruler if the old succession hadn't been changed. It should be the same line of descent as the House of M'nos, because the first M'nos married the Daughter of Kariatu and the M'nos is the husband of the eldest daughter of the last M'nos. But apparently it isn't; sometime during the centuries that the House of M'nos has ruled the lines diverged. I don't know how."

She nodded. "I do. My great-great-grandfather put his son on the throne in defiance of the law. The next M'nos passed the throne on to the husband of his own daughter, but by the Old People's reckoning, the true line of descent was through that daughter that was passed over when my great-great-grandfather insisted on having his son succeed him. Apparently the girl refused to marry her brother; that's the way some other M'noses got their sons to succeed them."

It was my turn to nod my understanding. This I had learned from some of the stories I had been told by Aunt Brit. Now Akama gave me a real surprise.

"Do you know that your grandmother is the Daughter of Kariatu?"

I replied slowly. "No…no. But somehow when I remember the respectful way she was always treated by people of the Old Blood I'm not surprised. And I'm not surprised she didn't tell anyone except perhaps

P'sero, her husband. She's even more close-mouthed than the others of the Old People."

Akama looked thoughtful. "Close-mouthed to outsiders, yes. But they tell each other things. They know that your father is dead. Since he died while your grandmother was still alive this makes you the Son of the Daughter of Kariatu by their reckoning. And your borthers and sisters don't count because they weren't conceived and born in Kaphtu."

I looked at her in surprise. "Akama, what are you trying to tell me?" She looked very serious as she replied. "Ducalion, if you reckon descent from father to son as the Danaans do, you should be the ruler of Kaphtu, since you are the son of the only true son M'nos left. If you reckon descent as the Old People do, you are the rightful ruler of Kaphtu as the Son of the Daughter of Kariatu. If you married me, you'd be ruler of Kaphtu by ordinary Kaphtui law, as soon as my father died. None of these things is important in one way. I'm sure you didn't come to Kaphtíu looking for a throne, and I didn't fall in love with you because of what S'tono told me. No wait—don't say anything yet. Yes, I did fall in love with you and I want you to know it. But I have the same burden that every Ariadne has. The man I marry will be the ruler of Kaphtu, and I must choose the right man. If I didn't think you were the right man to rule Kaphtu, I'd have to try to keep my love a secret. But I think you're the man who could heal the wounds of this country."

I looked into her eyes, my heart pounding. "Akama, I've loved you since the first day on the practice field. I'd give anything to marry you. But as for being ruler of Kaphtu, the thought seems mad. I'm just a sea trader."

She smiled and stepped into my arms. "What do you think our ancestors were, Ducalion? What do you think built this House? My father is ruining Kaphtu because he cares nothing for the land or the trade. But right now I've had enough of politics…"

Our first embraces were awkward enough, but so delightful as to drive all other thoughts out of our minds for a long time. But presently my srong-willed darling returned to unfinished business. "Ducalion, my love, there are a lot of things you left out of what you told me…"

I smiled and gathered her more comfortably in my arms. "All right, love, but now you have to be prepared for some surprises. To start with, your Aunt Ariadne isn't dead. She's living very happily in the Bright Land with her husband, Dionysius, and their children…"

It was a long story, and I was glad that she could know that I was telling the truth. Most people say sincerely enough that they believe in the gods—they listen to the sacred stories, perform the prescribed rituals—but at any hint that the Olympians are active here and now, that they or someone they know might come into contact with them, they show a curious kind of skepticism. I think it is partly fear, a dislike of the idea that powerful and uncontrollable beings might interfere with *their* lives. Even Akama felt it to some extent. As I told her of Britomartis and Ariadne and Dion she hung on my words, fascinated. But when I came to my meeting with Apollo she showed not fear but the anger that was her defensive reaction to danger.

"But what does he want with you? Why is he poking around Kaphtu? What does he mean to do?"

I held her hands as I gave her the unpalatable truth about the Olympians. "My dear, whatever he means to do we can't stop him. He's not answerable to us, or to anyone except Zeus and the King beyond the Kings. The Olympians are just in their own fashion, but their fashion isn't always ours. Our plans will have to fit in with his, whatever they are. The best way to think of the Olympians is as you think of the sea or the weather: be grateful when they favor you and ride it out if they turn on you. Just don't think you can control them."

She considered me. "My father thinks there's nothing he can't control. It's part of his strength. It gives him tremendous confidence and force. It's also his greatest weakness. When he finds something he can't control he tries to ignore it or forget it. He did that about Ariadne leaving him and now I see why you've told me the whole story. But a good ruler has to face facts—as you do."

I smiled and shook my head. If Akama would marry me that was enough. I had no real belief that I would ever rule Kaphtu. If she wanted a throne I might even be able to offer her that of Karia. Riadamantes ruled without a queen, and Lykos and Aphea had no children other than Britomartis. It was uncertain what would happen when they all died, but there was no great enthusiasm in Karia for simply bringing Riadamantes's heir from Kaphtu to take the throne. Strange as it seemed, with the death of my father I had become First Councillor of the kingdom. I was a definite possibility for the throne of Karia when Riadamantes died. But in my present mood I would have welcomed the opportunity to carve out a kingdom as Riadamantes had, to lay it at the feet of Akama.

There was a knock on the door then—one of Akama's older ladies on some invented pretext. In fact, she was just reminding us of the proprieties. For me to be alone with Akama even for the few minutes we had taken would surely set tongues wagging. In one sense that didn't matter; for both Akama and me our eventual marriage was a settled thing, it was just a matter of fighting to make it a reality. Akama and I had both had to fight for things before, she perhaps more than I, and we had never wanted anything as we wanted this. I was a little tempted to ask Apollo when I met him again what would happen to us. In my own mind I was certain that we would marry, but I was afraid to trust my intuitions where my own fears or desires were concerned.

That I would see Apollo again I knew without any need for intuitions. He had said he wanted me to do something for him. For an Olympian to admit that meant that he wanted something very much; where their own desires are concerned the Olympians are not easily discouraged. But what on earth could a mortal do for an Olympian? Since I would learn that when he was ready to tell me and not before, I put it out of my mind and concentrated on getting ready for our first Dance.

Apollo's words had encouraged me to take my own hunches about the future a little more seriously and I found that I could anticipate the bull's moves well enough to give me a little extra edge in the jumping. For, or course, even when the bull is well under control of the Tauromath there is some uncertainty about his motions. When you work with the same bull long enough you learn to anticipate his moves. I was using my little bit of Power to shortcut the learning process.

By the time of our first Dance, Akama had the bull as well under control as most Tauromaths ever have him. Britomartis or Ariadne could have done better, but even before they had joined the Olympians both of them had an amount of Power unusual for a mortal. The other male Leaper did a creditable Roll Under, and as he learned to trust Akama's control of the bull he was able to do a good side leap. The other female Leaper was quick and competent at ordinary side leaps, but she was not an inspired Leaper. I doubted whether she would ever go over the horns in a head leap.

At any rate, we had little time for training; the first Dance of the season was almost upon us. The first Dance is part of a festival which celebrates the beginning of the season in which it is safe to sail the seas. It said much about the decline of Kaphtui sea-trading that it was as late as this, and that Syrian ships were already sailing the seas before any Kaphtui ships were launched.

With so little time left, there was little we could do to improve the performance of the other Leapers. Akama was already good and her improved control over the bull was helping her to relax and concentrate on her own leaping. That left me, and I very much wanted the first performance of Akama's Dancers to be spectacur, not merely creditable. So there was nothing for it but for me to try to master the head leap. The few times that I had worked with a real bull before coming to Kaphtu had been with Aunt Brit or Ariadne in control of the bull and my mother leaping along with them. All three of them seemed to float over the bull's horns with scarcely any effort, but when I had tried it a few times I realized the strength and coordination needed to grasp the bull's horns as you ran to meet his charge, let his head toss lift you off your feet and then control your movement so you landed squarely on the bull's back, ready to do a handspring off of his rump to dismount. I had managed a few passable leaps under the critical eye of my mother and her Olympian friends, but it was another thing to reach in a few days of practice a standard high enough to make a good showing in the Dance itself. The only way to do it was by constant practice in the time we had left. The bull thundered down the practice field time after time with the other two Leapers practicing side leaps or the Roll Under as often as they cared to, but with the main purpose of each run being to allow Akama and me to perfect a double head leap.

The basic drill was for me to stand beside Akama, then as the bull reached the right point in his charge run toward him for my first head leap. As soon as I landed I would turn and Akama would follow me over. I would touch hands with her in the steadying gesture that is really unnecessary if the leap is well done. She would wheel and turn the bull with her control over him. As he started back toward us first Akama and then I would run to him and do a second head leap. This was difficult enough, but as we mastered the basic routine we tried to cut the time between our leaps, so that from the time of my first leap to the time of her last one there was a continuous flow of action. Well done, this would look very fine indeed, but the timing was so close that even a small slip could make it not only awkward but dangerous.

Akama had no difficulty with the leaps themselves, but it is hard to do two things at once, and her leaps distracted her from her control of the bull, as the necessity of controlling the bull distracted her from full concentration on her leaps. The only way for her to do both was to make the pattern so nearly automatic that she hardly had to think of what she was doing, and constant practice was the only way to do that.

If neither of us had had anything else to worry about in the Dance, our own leaps would have been work enough, but Akama had to be sure the other Leapers' moves were coordinated with ours and I had to learn the intricate pattern of steps that constituted the Dance proper, to which our leaps were only embellishments. Both of us lost weight in these last days before the Dance, and Akama was beginning to look drawn.

At last, the afternoon before the Dance, Akama called a halt. She sent the other Dancers to rest and told the handlers to turn our bull out to pasture. A few quick orders to the palace servants produced cloaks for us both and a basket, which she handed to me. Then she took my hand, and without returning to the palace, we walked slowly up a trail that climbed gradually up the slopes of Juktas, the low rocky mountain which could be seen from the palace. After the precisely

Richard Purtill

patterned physical efforts of the Dance, our slow
ambling pace was a relaxation in itself, although I had
to keep shifting the basket from hand to hand because
my arms and shoulders ached from the constantly
repeated head leaps.

We climbed past vineyards and olive groves, the
ground gradually getting rockier and less arable. Then
there was pasture for sheep and goats and finally
nothing but rocks and small scrubby bushes. As the
path curved around a pile of rocks, Akama took a
hidden side trail and suddenly we walked through a
narrow opening into a tiny valley, totally hidden in a
fold of the mounain. A tiny stream wound down the
center of the valley and though the ground was still
rocky the stream and the shade encouraged greenery.
The place was a paradise of grass and flowering
shrubs, with a large flowering tree standing near the
entrance and another at the head of the valley.

Akama led me to a grassy slope where the stream
fell a few feet, making a little waterfall, and sat down.
I lay down at her feet on the grass and stretched out my
tired body. "This is one of my few pieces of self-
indulgence," Akama's voice came from above my
head. "An earthquake opened a crack many years ago
and the grass and trees grew up. I used my authority as
a priestess of Ria to declare it a shrine to the goddess.
Otherwise the peasants would have pastured their
beasts here and the greenery would have never
survived. I use it as a retreat when I can't stand the
palace anymore."

I opened my eyes and looked at her face, upside down from where I lay at her feet. "Why did you bring me here, Akama?"

She smiled tenderly and leaned over and rumpled my hair. "Not for lovemaking, my dear, we're both too tired. And I don't intend to get pregnant before the end of this years Dances. Just to talk and relax, as we couldn't do in the palace. There's food and wine in the basket, and we won't be missed at the palace for a few hours, not by anyone who matters. Some of my servants know where I am, but they won't talk. Ducallion, do you think we can do it tomorrow?"

I shut my eyes again and flopped my hands out on the grass, palms up. "I honestly don't know, my dear. With more practice we could do it easily. But there's no more time for practice. Do you want to fall back on a simpler routine?"

She shook her head. "I'd rather try and fail than give up without trying. We can do it if everything goes just right."

I lay back, content to leave the decision to her. We talked quietly of other things for awhile, and presently ate a light meal from the basket, washed down with wine mixed with the clear cold water from the stream. We were both half dozing when there was a sound from the bushes at one side of the little valley. We could see bushes wave, but nothing came out of them. I raised myself on one elbow to look, not expecting danger in a valley that had been peaceful ever since we entered it, and Akama, who was a little less tired than I, got up and walked over to the bushes.

"A kid or lamb must have strayed in and got caught," she said over her shoulder. "They do occasionally. I should put something across the entrance when we leave."

Suddenly something in the way the bushes were moving gave me an uneasy feeling. The motion was too regular to be caused by an animal thrashing about. I caught a glimpse of a rope going up the side of the valley from the bushes, almost invisible against the greenery on the side of the valley. I sprang to my feet then and raced after Akama just in time to see the first rocks spilling down the slope. I would never reach her in time.

"The tree," I shouted. "Get behind the tree." As she heard my voice Akama sprang for the all-too-slender trunk of the flowering tree at the end of the valley. I saw her fingers touch the trunk just as the whole end of the valley seemed to collapse in an avalanche of dirt and rock, burying her body and most of the tree itself under a pile of stones.

Chapter Six
THE SUBSTITUTE

I hurled myself on the pile of stones, clawing frantically at it with my bare hands, but as the dust settled I saw that I would never shift that jumbled heap of rock and dirt and broken shrubs and branches—not in time to help Akama. I kept clawing away, but my mind and heart concentrated on a mental cry for help with every ounce of my being behind it. "Aunt Brit, Aunt Brit," I was sobbing under my breath. I gave a great sigh of relief as a familiar golden sparkle filled the air, but it was Ariadne, not Britomartis, who appeared. For the moment it was enough that it was an Olympian. "Akama. She's caught under that pile of rock," I gasped.

She nodded. "Get back, K'demus," she said in a low, urgent voice. "You'll only be in the way." I stepped back reluctantly and Ariadne began pushing the rocks away as if they had been a pile of pillows. A small rock hit my leg with enough force to draw blood, but I scarcely noticed it; I was sobbing with mixed relief and apprehension. In what seemed hours but was only moments Ariadne had uncovered Akama, crouched at the base of the tree and partly protected from the rock fall by its trunk. But she was still and pale and there was blood on her face and limbs. Ariadne lifted her as easily as if she had been a truss of straw and carried her over to the grassy bank where we had eaten.

"She's alive," said Ariadne exultantly. "The tree saved her from the worst. Wet the cloth, K'demus, and wipe off the blood so I can see what I'm doing."

I seized the cloth that had covered the food, wet it in the stream and sponged Akama's face gently. My heart bounded as her lips moved and she gave a faint moan.

Ariadne's hands followed mine as I sponged and she murmured to me as I worked. "Her skull's not fractured...bruising but I can take care of that...collarbone all right...this nipple was crushed, but I can restore it...take off her belt and kilt, K'demus...no internal damage...ah, here's the worst, this leg is broken in two places." She touched Akama's head and the injred girl, whose eyelids had been fluttering, sighed and sunk deep into unconsciousness.

"All right, K'demus, this will be the hardest for you. I'll relax the muscles and you must pull her leg straight. You'll feel the bones grate, but don't worry, she won't. All right, a little more. Now let it go back just a little...hold still!"

A slight burst of golden light came from between Ariadne's palms and seemed to sink into Akama's leg. Ariadne stepped back and looked down at her. Akama might have fallen asleep on the grass after washing in the stream. Her skin glowed with health and she was completely relaxed. I was suddenly acutely aware of her nakedness and her desirability. I covered her gently with one of the cloaks we had brought.

Ariadne smiled and passed her hand over Akama's brow. Her eyes opened and looked into mine. "Ducalion, I had the strangest dream..." she began, and then her eyes widened with surprise as she saw Ariadne.

"It wasn't a dream, Akama," I said gently. "Ariadne saved you. This is your mother's sister, Akama, whose amulet you've been wearing."

She gave a little frown and shook her head. "It can't be. Ariadne is older than my mother and she's not much older than I. And Ariadne is...no longer in this world..." She stopped and her eyes showed that she had realized the truth.

Ariadne nodded and smiled at her tenderly. "Yes, I'm your aunt, Akama. I've been living in a world where there is no aging or death, but for all that, I'm a wife and mother and perhaps a little older and wiser than I look. Your Ducalion called me in time and I was able to heal your wounds, but you've had a bad shock and you'd better keep off that leg as much as possible for a night and a day." Our faces must have shown our feelings for she understood immediately. "You have a Dance tomorrow," she said and it was a statement, not a question. We nodded, almost in unison and her face grew thoughtful. "There are things I could do to delay the Dance, but they might hurt innocent people. K'demus, does your Akama look as much like me as I think she does?"

I stared at her, half guessing her plan. "You're very much ailke," I said, "but..."

Ariadne waved aside difficulties with a gesture. "Illusion will take care of the rest," she said. "It's easy when there's something real to build on." She knelt down by Akama's side. "Akama, may I take your place tomorrow?" she asked gravely. "I'll take good care of your Dancers."

Akama nodded slowly, her eyes on Ariadne's. "Yes, oh yes. I'd be honored. I'd never be ready to Dance anyway without your seal stone."

Ariadne almost grinned. "Ah yes, my old seal," she said. "I had better borrow it back for awhile. We cheated a little over that." We looked at her, puzzled, and she smiled again as she explained, "Ducalion's mother strictly forbade us to help her son unless it was a real emergency. But we've been keeping an eye on things and when we saw the trouble you were having with the bull, Akama, I put my seal stone in the old chest in my room. I'm glad it helped."

I looked at her a little suspiciously. "What else did you do?" I asked.

She shook her head gravely. "We had nothing to do with your meeting with 'Pollo," she said. "We have no idea of what he's doing in Kaphtu. None of the other Olympians had seen him in quite awhile, and we won't tell them where he is until we find out what this is all about—oh, I told Dion, of course."

"You keep saying we…" I began.

Ariadne smiled. "Brit and I are doing this together, of course," she said. "You were calling for her really just now, I know, but I was closer. She's with your mother at the moment." In answer to my unspoken question she went on. "Your mother is safe and well. Our Dance helped her, and she's beginning to accept your father's death. At times she's almost her old self. She is even quarreling with me as she used to, which is one reason Brit is there and I'm here. But it's a good sign; she was too quiet and agreeable at first. I haven't known her to be so quiet since she was pregnant with you, Ducalion."

Akama looked at her. "You knew Ducalion's mother before he was born," she said slowly, "but you still look like a girl…"

Ariadne shook her head gently. "Try not to dwell on things like that, my dear. We are different from you. I never knew it more clearly than when I saw Alceme mourning for her husband. There is a great gulf between mortal and immortal, but love can bridge it. Pretend I'm your older sister. Your mother and I were never as close as we should have been, perhaps you and I can do better."

Akama smiled but she yawned in the middle of her smile and Ariadne became brisk. "I don't know how long you think you can get away with being out alone with Ducalion, my dear, but certainly not after dark. We'd better get to work. In a few minutes I'm going to put you to sleep, and as I do it I'll look at some things from the surface of your mind—names and faces of those that I'll meet while I'm taking your place, that sort of thing. I won't go any deeper than I can help. I don't want to intrude too much on your privacy. First I want you to see the guardians I'll set about you so you won't be afraid when you see them in the morning."

Ariadne lifted her hand in a gesture curiously like the bull-summoning gesture Akama had used the day we met. From the shadows of the greenery against the valley wall there stepped out a little group of figures, male and female. The women could almost have been human, though they were a little too tall and slender and graceful. But the male figures had broad-nosed alien faces, and a tail like a horse's tail hung from each tanned back, growing out just above the buttocks. Their silence was the watchful silence of wild things, but at Ariadne's beckoning gesture they came toward us, bringing with them strangeness and mystery that hung about them like a mist.

As they stood watching silently, Ariadne slipped casually out of her robe and tossed it to Akama, who suddenly looked at me and blushed, reminded of her own nakedness by Ariadne's. But Ariadne herself was totally unconcerned. I remembered my mother telling me that one sign of an Olympian, male or female, was an indifference to nudity. "To be naked and unashamed is the mark of a god—or a beast," the proverb goes. Ariadne knelt by Akama for a moment, looking into her eyes, then straightened up and found Akama's kilt and belt where I had tossed them. She grimaced at the blood and dirt on the kilt and rinsed it in the stream before putting it on. Akama was half asleep as I kissed her and lay the cloak over her. I saw that she still wore her seal and I pulled the delicate chain over her head and handed it to Ariadne, who put it on her own neck.

Ariadne made a little disapproving sound when she noticed the chain. "I should have changed this," she said. "It's Hephaestus's work; no mortal ever made flinks so fine, not even Daedalus." She smiled at Akama. "Sleep now, my dear, and rest tomorrow. Ducalion and I may not be able to get back until late tomorrow, but by that time you'll be as good as new. No one will get near this valley with the Wild Ones on guard, and they'll bring you food when you want it.

They'll understand you if you speak simply, and you may even get them to speak to you if you're patient and don't frighten them." Akama was already asleep as Ariadne led the way out of the valley and down the slope. I was never surprised at anything the Olympians knew, but I wondered if Ariadne had taken knowledge of this path from Akama's mind or if she had known this valley when she had lived in the Palace.

At the moment, though, there were more urgent problems on my mind. "Someone made that avalanche fall on Akama," I said. "Is she safe with only those Wild Ones for a guard if they come back in force?"

She smiled a little grimly and said, "Oh yes. The Wild Ones are dwellers in the Bright Land; in fact, they're children of the Olympians. They don't have our power but they can deal with mortals easily enough. They can send the Fear if they need to, but that's not their only weapon." She paused a moment and said grimly," I sent a group of them after those who sent down that rockslide. They'll hunt them through the woods and hills until they're exhausted and then hound them into N'sos. It will be for Akama to decide what to do with them."

I shuddered a little at the thought of that wild hunt through the waste places and stopped worrying about Akama's safety. I stumbled on the path as Ariadne set a fast pace down the slope and she wheeled and took my arm, looking into my eyes.

"You have been practicing hard, haven't you, Ducalion? Here, eat some of this." She put some flat cakes into my hand and I munched on them as we walked along more slowly now. They had a wholesome, slightly sweet flavor. When Ariadne saw that I had finished she stopped again and lay both hands on my shoulders. "Close your eyes, Ducalion. I'm going to give you some of my power; the ambrosia you've just eaten will help you to make use of it. I can't give you too much power now or you won't sleep tonight, but I'll give you more in the morning if you need it.

Warmth seemed to flow down her hands and fill my body and suddenly the fatigue of the past days of grueling practice fell from me. I felt as strong and fit as I ever had in my life.

Ariadne looked into my eyes and nodded. "Enough but not too much, I think. Yes. Your mother was very strict about not making you dependent on us."

I grinned, suddenly feeling buoyant and confident. "I don't know why you and Aunt Brit let my mother give you orders."

Ariadne answered me very seriously. "They're very wise orders, K'demus. Friendship between an Olympian and a mortal is a very difficult thing. Your mother and Lykos both know when to accept our help and when to refuse. We respect their decisions. When an Olympian deals with a mortal it's easy to—break things—without meaning to. The mortal has to set the pace. Most are afraid of us and want nothing to do with us. Those that aren't afraid often get greedy. But we aren't all-powerful. Sooner or later the greedy ones want something we can't give. Lykos wants nothing but to live a good life with 'Phea. Your mother has never asked for much from us, but what she asked was always sensible. She was always a practical girl."

I smiled again at that and would have said more but we were drawing near the palace, and even on the little trail we were following we began to meet people. We fell silent until we reached the foot of the West Staircase in the Great Court, then Ariadne turned to face me again and said in a low voice, "No one has noticed us up to now; they've looked at us but not seen us. That's easier than either illusion or true invisibility. Only now I have to be seen as Akama. Look at me and think of her—think of the differences between us. Tell me when you can't see any difference between me and your image of her."

It was uncanny to watch her face and form change before my eyes and become that of Akama, but there was something in the smile she turned on me as we parted that was still Ariadne. "You'll sleep well tonight," she said in Akama's voice, and I did.

Dancers of each sex no longer shared a common sleeping room as they had in my mother's time. I went straight to my little private cubicle and fell asleep, I'll swear, in the act of lying down on my bed.

The Dance the next day might have been an anticlimax, but it wasn't, of course. No matter how much you have practiced it, the Dance itself on the bark-covered Great Court, with every available vantage point filled with spectators, is like nothing else in the world. No practices are ever held in the court itlsef. Covering the paving stones with shredded bark and cleaning it afterwards is too big a job to be done often, and the court is usually the focus of the whole life of the palace—too busy a place to be closed for practice sessions. The practice court south of the palace was just the same size and shape as the court, however, and the passageway of logs from which the bulls are released in practice is the same width and length as the awkward corridor of the South Gate up to which the bull must be led for the Dance.

Ariadne was doing nothing which Akama would have difficulty duplicating later, so we Dancers filed into the corridor first, letting the handlers bring the bull behind us. Both Britomartis and Ariadne, when they were Tauromaths, had taken the bull down the corridor themselves, with the Dancers in line behind the bull, although very few Tauromaths have that much control of their bulls.

The flutes and drums were already sounding the first measures of the Dance and the Dancers moved straight onto the court with hardly a pause. As soon as we were clear of the door, the handlers let the bull come out and stood there holding him until the first measures of the Dance were over.

We advanced with the ancient intricate steps, two lines weaving in and out toward the thrones at the north end of the court. The king's throne was occupied by Theseus's viceroy, an elderly Athenian with sharp features and eyes that gave nothing away, and the queen's throne by the equally elderly priestess of Ria. We saluted the thrones and Ariadne and I wove back through the Dance to the bull. Ariadne was of course in perfect control, but I saw tension on S'tono's face as he loosed the bull for her to take. He at any rate had no suspicion that this was not Akama, and he was still uncertain of Akama's powers. Again there was the slow progress down the court to "present the bull to the thrones." In the old days this had been done immediately, without the initial progress of the Dancers alone up the court, but the Dance had been elaborated since my mother's day.

As we moved up the court leading the bull, I saw a movement at one of the few windows that was not crowded with spectators—an awkward little window that only commanded a view of part of the court, It was the hard-faced man I had met on the streets of Anmisos. He had a short bow in his hands with the arrow already half drawn back. He was waiting for us to come a little closer before he shot his arrow.

Chapter Seven
ARIADNE'S DANCE

I was holding one horn of the bull and Ariadne the other. When I saw the hard-faced man I must have made some motion the bull felt, and mind -linked to the bull as she was, Ariadne was aware of it. By the time I glanced over at her, she was already searching the crowd with her eyes to see what had startled me. When she spotted the man with the bow her face grew grim. For an instant, I could see a faint circle of lights like stars over her head. Her eyes flashed dark fire and the man at the window clutched his chest and slid down out of sight behind the sill of the window. The arrow, released by his hand and powered by the half-drawn string, clattered against the side of the window and fell back into the room, but the noise attracted attention, and by the time we had passed the window a palace guard was already forcing his way through the crowd to a stairway. I didn't know if Ariadne had killed the man or merely rendered him unconcious, but his lifeless or senseless body would be discovered before the Dance was over.

I had hardly had time to recover from this before we had saluted the thrones again and led the bull back through the Dance and were making our way back to position for our first leaps. In my mother's day, the practice for the Dance was regarded as an entertainment but the Dance itself was a sacred ceremony, solemn but surprisingly brief. The bull would usually only do two runs; one to the thrones and then back to his handlers at the door by which he had entered, with each dancer doing one leap on each run. Only on some special occasion, such as the last Dance of the year, would there be more runs and more leaps.

But in the years since Theseus had become king at Kaphtu the old Kaphtui culture had been affected by Athenian attitudes, and one result of this was that the Dance had become more a spectacle and less a religious ceremony. The crowds would have felt cheated by fewer than four runs of the bull, and more runs than that were not uncommon. Akama and I had planned for four runs, and Ariadne was keeping strictly to what had been practiced. When Ariadne signaled the handlers to release the bull, he broke into a charge almost immediately. This is what normally happens. In practice you sometimes have difficulty getting the bull to charge rather than just trot, but in the Dance itself the bull is excited by the crowd and only too eager to charge.

The sallow-skinned girl Leaper did an elegant side leap as the bull passed her. Like many girl Leapers, she looked a little angular and bony but was extremely graceful when Leaping. Then the other male Leaper and I did the hornswing: each of us ran toward the bull at an angle, grasped the horn on our side and did a swing on the horn which ended in a tumbler's roll on the ground. This drops the bull's head and slows him, making it easier for the lead Dancer, who is usually the Tauromath, to do a head leap. Ariadne had no need of such help, but Akama might have found it useful, since the bull was fresh and excited by its unfamiliar surroundings.

Ariadne did the head leap well, but no better than Akama would have done. Her style was exactly Akama's style, and I wondered if she had taken Akama's mannerisms from my mind or Akama's own. Ariadne then ran diagonally to the side of the court, just opposite me, turning the bull with her mind as she went. By the time the bull had turned, well short of the thrones, and got up speed on his backward charge, we were set for our simultaneous side leaps—a straight handstand over the bull's back, with only a slight check at the top point of the leap.

The other two Leapers then did a similar simultaneous side leap with a longer check at the top. In fact, they supported themselves on their hands, bodies perperndicular to the ground for several heartbeats, while the bull carried them a long spear's length down the court, Ariadne turned the bull again, and as it came back up the court the other male Leaper did a Roll Under the bull's hoofs; passing under the bull's belly after its front hooves had passed and before its rear hooves came up. The other girl Leaper had mounted a low ramp made of packed earth at the side of the court, and as the bull passed her did a leap clear over the bull's back, without touching it, ending in a handstand on the ground. This looks more difficult than it is, since you do not touch the bull at all and do not have to take his momentum into account. It can only go wrong if you leap too sooon and get snagged on the bull's horns. Mean bulls not fully under control have been known to slow down deliberately to try to catch someone doing the Leap Over.

We were now ready for the really difficult part of our Dance. As soon as the girl Leaper was over the bull, I moved into his path and ran toward him for my first head leap. Ariadne came over practically on my heels, turned the bull and set herself for her third and final head leap. As soon as we had touched hands, I wheeled and ran down the court to take position for my second head leap, running for the bull as soon as Ariadne was lifted by the bull's head toss.

This second leap of mine was the one that we had had the most trouble with in practice sessions, since the bull had to drop his head again just after tossing one Dancer over, and then give a good toss. A bull is strong, of course, but a head leap is a strain on his muscles as well as the Dancer's, and this was the fourth toss he had to do in rapid succession. With Ariadne in control his head was just in the right position and his toss just strong enough. As I landed, I realized with a lift of my heart that I had finished my part in my first Dance, and done creditably.

We could have ended with the spectacular double head leap, but the other two Leapers had wanted to do their part, so as the bull galloped back to the exit they did a side leap and Roll Under, coordinated so that he went under the bull just as she went over. Again this was easier than it looked, but it looked good and made a good finale for the Dance.

Really all that happens after this is that the fourteen Dancers file off the court; the non-leaping Ground Dancers first and then the Leapers. This is the chance for the crowd to express its enthusiasm, and I was pleased to hear that the name they were shouting was

Akama's. In fact, after a moment they began chanting in unison, "A-ka-ma, A-ka-ma." This kind of chanting is a traditional sign of great enthusiasm. Akama would be disappointed to have missed her first Dance, but we had achieved one major objective: to make her a favorite with the people. The Kaphtui will forgive a ruler almost anything if he or she is a great Dancer. I wondered how much of Theseus's unpopularity was due to the fact that although he had started to train as a novice, he had never gotten to his first Dance. His fight with Astariano and his flight to Athens had come first.

As we entered the corridor, where the bull was already being led away by the handlers, we were all jubilant. Ariadne gave a quick warm speech, in exactly Akama's manner, praising all of us for our success. But she went on. "I know it's usual to have a party just after the Dance to celebrate. But I also know how hard we've all been practicing. I think we'd all fall asleep at our own party. Rest up tonight and we'll have a party tomorrow that none of you will ever forget, I promise you. I want to see you, S'tono, and you, Ducalion, for just a moment and then I'll let you go get your rest, too."

As soon as the others were out of earshot, Ariadne said in a low tone to S'tono, "There was a man at a window with a bow, trying to shoot at the Dancers. He was struck down for his impiety by the gods, but I want to know who was behind him. Find out his name from the guards, someone will have identified him by now. Then find out from the palace servants where he was living. The servants always know that sort of thing. If you can, search his room and bring me

78

anything out of the way you find there. Use my name and authority if you have to, but avoid bringing me into it if you can."

S'tono grinned and nodded. A good many of the palace servants and guards were of the Old People and he was probably an excellent choice to get this kind of information. Again I wondered how much Ariadne had taken from Akama's mind and how much was her own familiarity with the palace and its workings.

As soon as S'tono was gone, Ariadne turned and smiled at me. I saw that she looked like herself again instead of like Akama. "No one is seeing us, just as no one did when we came from the valley. My masquerade is over, and it's time we got back to Akama. I hope she doesn't feel too badly about missing her Dance. I rather enjoyed being Mistress of the Dance again, myself."

As we made our way out of the palace I asked uneasily, "Do you really mean that people can't see us? They seem to look at us, get out of our way…"

Ariadne smiled. "Haven't you seen someone you know and not recognized him because you were preoccupied or because you saw him in unexpected surroundings? This is like that. I keep their recognition response from working. They see us, they even see us as we actually are, they just don't recognize us as ourselves, or think about us at all. They wouldn't know me, of course, but after today's Dance you could hardly go anywhere near N'sos without being recognized."

She paused a moment and then went on. "You're beginning to look a great deal like my foster father,

K'demus, do you know that? And Akama is very like me as a girl. She's had a hard time, perhaps harder in some ways than I did, but I think she's come out of it very well. Her servants love her and that's always a good sign. I hope you'll find happiness together, but there are greater difficulties in your way than you can guess now. For one thing, Theseus sin't going to like the idea of his daughter choosing her own husband. It would be simple enough if you could just take her back to Karia, but she won't abandon her responsibilities as the Ariadne. I know, I've been in a very similar position myself."

I nodded somberly. "I know. She talks of marrying me and our ruling Kaphtu together but I don't see how that's possible. And she's not a girl to run out on her responsibilities—either the Dance or the succession to the throne. I have a feeling that we'll be united eventually but I see lots of trouble first. The only thing to do is to take it one day at a time and do the best we can. Somehow the problems with Theseus and Akama worry me less, though, than this business with Apollo."

Ariadne looked very thoughtful. "I've never pretended to understand the Olympians—the real ones, that is; I always feel that I'm somehow an imposter. You've got to remember that all of the children of Zeus by Titan women are only a quarter human. In many ways 'Pollo and his sister and Hermes are harder to understand than Zeus or Posudi or their sisters. 'Pollo has always seemed to have a disdainful attitude toward mortals, and toward Brit and Dion and me because we're half mortal. It's quite unlike him to be passing himself off as a mortal, or to be as friendly to you as he has been. There's something strange about all this."

I didn't need to be told that; I was grimly aware of it. But for the moment we had more immediate problems than what the Olympian wanted with me. The first was Akama's condition. My heart lifted when we entered the little hidden valley and she ran toward us without even a trace of a limp. There were flowers in her hair and her face was bright. The Wild Ones were nowhere in sight, but somehow I could feel their presence. The little valley seemed to be filled with the air of strangeness they brought with them. Even Akama looked a little alien, with her head garlanded with flowers, wearing Ariadne's dress.

"The Wild People were wonderful," she told Ariadne as soon as she came up to us. "It's like being able to make friends with the trees and streams. I can see why the country people are afraid of them. They're so strange and different. But I loved them."

Ariadne smiled and embraced her gently. "People who like animals often get on well with the Wild Ones," she said. "And people who love the beauty of the countryside. You're right, Akama, the Wild Ones are very close to the trees and waters. In the Bright Land such things seem alive themselves, and the Wild Ones often form a special kind of rapport with trees or streams there that somehow carries over to the counterparts of those things in this world. I suspect that the counterpart of this valley in the Bright Land is a special haunt of theirs."

Akama turned from Ariadne and came to my arms. We held each other in silence for a few moments, aware of Ariadne watching us benevolently, but somehow we were not self-conscious. Finally, she spoke, "I'm sorry to have to take you away from this peaceful valley. I wish you could stay here and rest awhile. But I think you'd better get back to the palace and go to bed. You have things to do tomorrow." She told Akama about the archer and about the orders she had given S'tono. "With luck he may be able to find something to confirm Ducalion's suspicions that the High King at Mykenae is behind these attacks on you. If you do find evidence you might use it to teach the young hotheads a lesson. They don't like Theseus's long-distance rule of Kaphtu, but they won't like being used as pawns by the Argives either."

Akama nodded grimly. "I'll hold a Tribunal," she said, "and summon everyone who we know has any connection with Rianisu. If I tried to move against them in other ways I'd have to go through my father's representatives, but anyone can call a Tribunal for good cause, and no one can dispute my right as the Daughter of the M'nos to sit in judgment at the Tribunal. I think the group is divided enough so that they'll talk, and if they talk, I can get at the truth."

Ariadne looked at her searchingly. "Yes," she murmured, "you have the power of Truth, don't you? It's one of the powers that comes down in the House of M'nos, along with Tauromathy. Use it wisely and you should be able to sort out this particular conspiracy. Then you'll still have plenty of troubles left. Call on me if you have to." She gave a final smile and lifted her hand, then she was gond. The valley seemed to become more ordinary as she vanished. I wondered if she had taken the Wild Ones with her back to the Bright Land.

Akama and I looked at each other a moment and sighed, then picked up our cloaks and the basket and started back to the palace. Akama was full of questions about the Dance and this topic lasted us almost till we got to the House. We no longer had an Olympian with us to let us walk unseen or unnoticed, so we had to come quietly to the practice field by little-used byways. There was no getting into the House itself without passing the guards, but since we had come from the direction of the practice field, it might be thought that we had been on business connected with today's Dance.

As we approached the South Gate Akama put her cloak around her despite the warmth of the evening. She was still wearing Ariadne's dress, and the Olympians usually seemed to dress more or less in the Danaan style, though the material was finer and softer than any mortal weave. Akama had Danaan dresses which she wore in Athens, but she had always made a point of wearing Kaphtui clothing when she was in Kaphtu. For her to come into the palace in a Danaan-style dress would cause questions, and those questions might lead to others even harder to answer.

She left the flowers in her hair, and as we passed the guards I saw a few half-concealed smirks among the guards. They thought we had been frolicking together in the meadows near the palace, no doubt. It was a good enough explanation of our absence since the Dance, and I wondered if Akama had left the flowers in her hair deliberately for that reason. But for once, I think, she was not planning or plotting, for when we reached the door of her rooms she pulled the garlands from her head and looked at them with an expression almost of tenderness.

"I wish…" she began. Suddenly there was a movement in the shadows farther down the corridor. I stepped in front of Akama, every muscle tense, but I relaxed when I saw S'tono's familiar face.

He had a small packet in his hand and he said quickly in a low voice, "I know you said to come in the morning, my lady, but I didn't dare keep these overnight. I found all of this concealed in the room of the man who tried to shoot at you." Glancing up and down the empty corridor nervously, he pulled back the cloth which covered the packet just enough for us to see that the packet was full of finely worked gold jewelry. There was the worth of many years' trading ventures in that little packet.

"That wasn't to buy ordinary mercenaries or allies," I said. "He must have been planning to bribe some very high official."

Akama was looking at each piece in turn, holding them up to the light which came from a nearby air shaft. "We're going to the craftsmen's quarters as soon as I change this dress," she said. "I have an idea about this jewelry. If I'm right it may be the evidence we need to link this conspiracy to the Argives."

Chapter Eight
THE TRIBUNAL

As we entered the main craftsmen's workroom a little later, I looked around me, full of curiosity. This had been the domain of Daedalus, the almost legendary master craftsman, in my mother's time. My mother had liked Daedalus, and had even in her self-interested way considered marrying him, before she met my father. But Daedalus had left Kaphtu not long after the Great Wave, and the master craftsman who deferentially ushered us into his private inner chamber was a dark, stocky Kaphtui, very young for his important position. Akama put the packet of jewelry in his hands and asked bluntly, "Can you identify these, Ph'tano?"

The craftsman spread the jewelry out on his workbench, examining each piece minutely. "It's old work, my lady," he said. "Some of it very old. All Kaphtui work but most of it not of the highest quality. Showy pieces mostly. I'm sure I've never seen any of them, and most pieces of valuable jewelry left in Kaphtu have been through my hands at one time or another, for repair or cleaning. Let me call old Iphano, my lady. He worked on jewelry in this palace before I was born."

Akama nodded and the old craftsman was called from his bench. He examoned the pieces as carefully as Ph'tano had, laying some of the pieces to one side after he had examined them. He looked at Akama with eyes that were still sharp despite the rheum of age and his thin voice was confident: "My lady, these pieces I have set aside I can swear to; the others I am fairly sure of. When the Argives raided us after the Great Wave we were ordered by the Lord Riatano to leave some jewelry in the palaces we abandoned, so that the raiders would be satisfied with their loot and return to the Argolid. We left mostly things that were flashy but not of the best workmanship. Just as well, because I've heard from traveling craftsmen that the Argives melted much of it down or hammered it out. They make gold death masks for their kings when they can get the gold. A lot of Kaphtíui gold went into Argive tombs." He went on slowly. "Some of this might have been traded, and passed from hand to hand. But this much all together…I think whoever you got this from, my lady, must have gotten it from the Argive kings."

Akama looked at him grimly…"I thought so," she said. "Would you swear to that before a Tribunal, Iphano?"

The old man met her gaze steadily. "Yes, my lady," he said confidently.

Akama turned to me. "Get some rest, Ducalion," she told me. "I'm calling a Tribunal tomorrow and I want you to sit with me as an assessor."

There were formalities to be observed, and it was late the next morning before the tribunal got under way. The hard-faced man had been dead when the guards found him. His body lay on a stretcher in the center of the court. Looking at that still form gave me an uneasy feeling: even Ariadne for all her kindness could be terrible enemy. Beside the body were the other results of Olympian power: the exhausted wretches who had operated the trap which had spilled the stones on Akama. They had staggered into the

palace early that morning, more afraid of whatever
invisible things pursued them than of the guards who
had been warned to expect them.

Behind the body and the exhausted men there stood
an uneasy crowd of young Kaphtui aristocrats; every
man who was known to be an associate of Rianisu's,
and Rianisu himself sitting uneasily on a bench, one
arm and one leg heavily bandaged.

The courtroom was of a pattern I was familiar with
from Karia, where Kaphtui laws prevailed. The
courtroom proper was a rectangular room with a door
in the middle of one of the long sides. Opposite the
door was a sort of balcony opening onto a smaller
room about the height of a tall man, above the floor of
the large room. Seated next to the balcony rail, Akama
could be seen from the room below, but I, seated a
little behind her, could hardly be seen unless I stood up
or came closer to the rail. In a complicated trial there
might be a whole staff of aides and advisors in that part
of the upper room, out of sight from the court. An
asssessor, or advisor to the judge, the role I was
playing, could, by sitting in just the right place a little
back from the judge, see into the court but remain
inconspicuous himself or herself, for the assessor was
usually a woman if the judge was a man, and a man if
the judge was a woman.

The Kaphtui rulers who had devised this form of
courtroom had a shrewd knowledge of human nature.
A defendant or witness in the courtroom had to look up
at the judge and speak loudly enough so that his or her
words could be heard, making it hard not to feel like a
suppliant before a god. The court officials stood or sat

below the balcony, facing the defendants or witnesses with their impassive scrutiny. Because they were just below the balcony, they could speak to the judge in quiet tones that could not be heard in the courtroom. Those before the court stood about in the middle of the room and the benches for spectators were behind them.

At a signal from Akama, the Summoner stepped slowly from the door to the wall just below the balcony, turned and crashed his staff of office to the floor three times. In his loud, unemotional herald's voice he gave the reasons for the calling of the Tribunal: the hard-faced man's attempt to shoot at the Dancers, the two exhausted wretches' attempt to kill or injure Akama with a rock fall. From the charge I learned for the first time the name of the hard-faced man: it was Archeopolis, Danaan for "ruler of a city." I wondered what his real rank and status had been and how he had come to Kaphtu.

Akama rose and gave the invocation to Ria, the Mother of the gods. This would normally be done by a court official, but as Holy One of Ria, Akama had precedence in any invocation of the Mother. As she finished, Akama nudged me and whispered, "Give the invocation for Posudi."

Like any sea captain, I am a priest of Posudi, and in fact the priesthood in our family is very old, going back from son to father to the earliest Pelasgians, the Sons of Posudi who had landed on Kaphtu and seized the rule from the Daughters of Kariatu. But we invoke only Zeus Labyriantos in our courts and it took me a moment to think how to adapt a seaman's prayer to a court situation.

The opening phrases were familiar ones; they rolled easily off my tongue.

"Blue-haired Posudi, Earthshaker, horsemaster you of the bronze trident,
You dwell in the foundations of the full-bosomed sea
For to your lot fell the Third Portion, the unfathomable deep.
Maintain the foundations of the world, Gracious One, and the ships that range the seas."

Now I had to adapt the prayer and I didn't know the phrases used in Kaphtui courts. I did the best I could with a phrase from the sailors' prayer and a phrase from the Karian court ritual.

"Bring. peace, health and honest prosperity to the land
Bring truth and justice to this tribunal.
Father of the Kaphtui."

There had been a sort of gasp of indrawn breath as I rose to give the invocation, immediately silenced for the prayer, but as I finished, a little murmur of sound arose in the court, people trying to whisper to their neighbors without disturbing the court. The Summoner's staff crashed down and there was silence again. Before I seated myself again I looked at the little group of aristocrats in the center of the room. Those who had been in the crowd that threatened me almost cringed as my eyes fell on them. I thought of Apollo's words, "Seeing you will remind them of…unpleasant things."

Akama began the proceedings by asking each of Rianisu's friends if he had been part of the conspiracy against her. Almost all of them said that they had not, but as they answered, Akama looked deeply into their eyes and waved them to the right or to the left. A few muttered with shamefaced looks that they had, and she left them in the center of the group. Before long, there were three groups in the center of the court. Those on the right looked confused and worried but not guilty, while those on the left tried to keep from meeting each other's eyes. As member after member of the conspiracy had been waved to the left they must have realized, if they did not already know, that Akama could tell that they were lying. Rianisu himself, pale but trying to keep his dignity, moved to stand with the group in the center though he had not been questioned.

Akama turned first to the group on the right. "You are excused, my lords," she said with a slight mocking edge in her voice. "In future watch the company you keep."

There was almost a rush to the door by the members of the group. None was so bold as to try to find a place on the packed spectators' benches and see what happened to his friends.

Rianisu's face grew a little paler and grimmer, but he must have known the quality of the men who had left, for he had not tried to involve them in his plans.

Now Akama began to call witnesses. S'tono testified to finding the jewelry in Archepolis's room, and the old craftsman Iphano swore to what he had told us, that the jewels were Argive loot and could only have come from the Argive kings. A palace servant identified Archeopolis as, "A Danaan gentleman in the service of the Lord Euphoros."

I shared the shock that ran through the court. Euphoros was a Danaan nobleman who was Theseus's civil administrator in Kaphtu. Unless the name was a coincidence, he was an old opponent of Aunt Brit's—a blustering fellow who had been one of the original Tribute of Fourteen and had been made leader of the Ground Dancers to salve his injured dignity after he had tried and failed to interfere with Aunt Brit's plans. I thought it was probably the same man, for Theseus had wisely used former Dancers from Athens as his representatives in Kaphtu.

Akama called Euphoros to the center of the court and asked him in the same ironic tone if he had any explanation for the activities of his protege. Euphoros paled and said in an agitated voice that he had been surprised and shocked to learn of Archepolis's activities. He tried to say more but Akama's dark eyes were boring into his and he fell silent, shifting his weight from foot to foot.

Akama spoke then, and there was no doubt as to which of the two had the authority now, whatever Theseus had ordered. "I believe that my father needs to know of what has happened here, my lord," she said. "Do me the favor of making yourself ready to leave for Athens to report to him—at once."

Euphoros saluted and almost staggered back to the front bench he had taken so proudly when he entered the court. I thought I had a good idea of what official the Argive loot had been intended to bribe.

Now Akama turned to the remaining friends of Rianisu and asked them one by one if they had known of the Argive involvement in the plot and of the plans to kill her. This time no one dared to lie to her, and she soon divided them into a shamefaced group on the left who had not known the depths of the plot, and a smaller group, frightened but still defiant, who had. She turned to the larger, less guilty, group first. "You were more fools than villains, my lords." Again there was irony in her voice, especially in her last words. "Those of you who will swear to be loyal to me and to Kaphtu in the future may go to your estates. Until the next Ship Festival do not show your faces in N'sos."

One by one they stepped forward and gave their oaths, leaving the court without looking at anyone's face. Even aside from the humiliation, the punishment was severe enough. They would spend the winter shivering in drafty country houses, cut off from the warmth and gaiety of N'sos. To a Kaphtui aristocrat the isolation would be as bad as prison.

Now Akama turned to the hard core of conspirators. Her voice seethed with contempt as she said, "You have lost the right to have your oaths taken seriously. You have lost the right to live in Kaphtu. Leave this land with what you can carry in your hands and on your backs. If you set foot on Kaphtui soil again you will die. This much mercy I grant you: eight years from now, the Great Year of the Olympians, you may sail into the harbor of Amnisos and send to me for permission to land and seek my forgivenesss.

According to your deeds in the interval I will decide. But for now, go, and take your dogs with you." She gestured to the whimpering wretches who had sprung the trap on her and watched stony-faced as they and the remaining conspirators were hustled from the court by the guards.

Her eyes turned to Rianisu, leaning, deadly pale, on his crutch beside the body of Archepolis. "Well, kinsman," she said, "I give you your choice. Will you swear loyalty and go to your estates for a year or will you leave Kaphtu?"

Rianisu earned my admiration as he straightened his injured body and said, "Lady, you have the gift of Truth. You will know I speak the truth when I say I was a tool of the others and knew nothing of the Argive gold or the plan to kill you. But I will not suffer less than the worst of my followers. For eight years I will tread the paths of exile and at the end of them I will come to ask your forgiveness." He saluted her and limped out of the court. I was not the only one who watched him go with regret. Alone of the conspirators he had left the court with some shred of honor.

At a gesture from Akama, guards took away the body of Archeopolis. Then she rose to her feet, and at the pressure of her hand I rose and stood beside her. "One thing remains to be done for the peace of Kaphtu," she said in the solemn tones of a priestess. "Here in the face of this assembly I pledge myself in marriage to the Lord Akademus, called Ducalion, Councillor of Karia, descendent of the House of M'nos, Son of the Daughter of Kariatu. The marriage will be accomplished after the last Dance this year.

Kaphtui, behold the man who will be your M'nos. Ariadne has spoken. The Tribunal is dismissed."

Chapter Nine
THE DOUBLE PATH

After that, of course, the party that Ariadne had promised the Dancers became a riotous celebration of our betrothal. The preparations for the Tribunal and the Tribunal itself had lasted nearly to the time of the evening meal and the celebration had been planned to start with a banquet, so Akama and I had no time for a real talk after the Tribunal. As the people filed out of the courtroom, Akama and I stepped to the back of the judges' room, out of sight of the court. She looked at me a little apprehensively, but I embraced her warmly enough to leave her no doubt that I was well pleased with what she had done. I don't know how long we clung together, but we were brought back to reality by the summoner tactfully making a clatter with his staff as he came up the stair to ask Akama to settle some details about the disposal of the prisoners. After that, Akama was absorbed in court business until it was time for her to dress for the banquet.

Late in the evening, when the meal had been cleared away and Dancers and their guests were drinking, laughing and talking together, Akama and I were able to slip out onto a balcony and talk quietly.

"It was partly a sudden impulse, of course. I saw that Euphoros was too worried about his own skin to think of making any protest on my father's behalf. And I remembered a story my mother told me once about two lovers who had been tried and acquitted before a Tribunal and married each other at the very Tribunal that had tried them." she told me.

By Kaphtui law a marriage takes place when two people declare in public their intention of living together permanently. It is usual but not necessary for the marriage to be blessed by a priestess of Ria the Mother. The person of higher rank, male or female, makes the declaration, and if the other party does not protest, he or she is taken to consent. I knew this, of course, but what Akama now told me was new to me.

"It turned out to be one of my better impulses," Akama said with a chuckle. "The summoner told me that a declaration of marriage before a Tribunal is a most solemn and binding kind of promise. According to him we're really married already. The consummation of the marriage is just a formality."

I laughed and took her into my arms, ignoring the amused glances of our friends, who could see us on the balcony from the room where the party was going on. "It won't be just a formality to me," I said.

In the days that followed we were to learn that the view of the palace officials, which soon became the view of everyone, was the same as that of the summoner. Akama and I were regarded as married and not just as betrothed. When and where we consummated the marriage was our own affair, though everyone knew that a Dancer could not risk getting pregnant at the beginning of the season. There was a belief that the power of Tauromathy was connected to virginity, and though Akama and I doubted this, we agreed that it would be foolish chances with either her control of the bull or her physical condition. Akama was as eager as I to make love, but we agreed reluctantly to wait until the night of the last Dance of the season.

So I kept my Dancer's cubicle for sleeping, but the conventions that had kept us from being alone together before our marriage no longer applied, and we spent most of the day in each other's company. There still plenty of need for practice but we had time now, for the second Dance of the season is not held until the first ship has returned from a mainland port. The ships set sail after the first Dance and have trade or other business to accomplish before they return. I was delighted to find that Akama's control over the bull was even better than it had been before the accident. She attributed this to the day she had spent in the company of the Wild Ones. By the time of the second Dance she would be able to do at least as well as Ariadne had done when she substituted, for Ariadne had held herself to what Akama could do at that time.

Successful Leapers are always popular heroes and heroines and this took care of any resentment there might have been at a stranger's appearing suddenly in Kaphtu and marrying the heiress. At times we were actually cheered by the crowds when we appeared together in public. We let the story of my parentage be known, and since my mother and Aunt Brit's other Dancers were almost legendary figures, this added to my own popularity. But I also found myself being treated with respect by hard headed merchants and palace officials who certainly not swayed by romance or Dance fever.

The merchants were pleased by the thought of having a sea-trader on the throne eventually. It was more important to them that I belonged to the merchant House of P'sero than that I was the son of a legendary Dancer or the grandson of the Daughter of Kariatu. The palace officials were impressed by the fact that I was from Karia. Despite the estrangement between the two countries, I found that Karia was regarded as a model of good government and that Riadamantes's justice was becoming a legend. They knew nothing of Lykos and Aphea, whom we Karians regarded as co - rulers, but Riadamantes was remered as the brother of the almost mythological Dark M'nos.

With Euphoros sent back to Athens, there was a lack of leadership. Akama took the reins firmly into her own hands, but I found that I was being looked to when she was not available. When S'tono called me "M'nosuma," I thought he was joking, but I soon heard the title from others. The syllable "ma" is diminutive in Kaphtui, and "M'nosuma" literally means "little M'nos" or "seed of a M'nos," but it is an old title for the heir apparent, the husband of the Ariadne who will be M'nos on the death of the reigning M'nos.

I had no great personal desire to be M'nos. I had been close enough to the throne in Karia to know that a good ruler is the servant of his people and the better ruler he is the more he is an overworked and under appreciated servant. Now I had to reckon with Akamaís sense of responsibility. She took her obligations as Ariadne very seriously and if I was to make her happy I would have to carry out those obligations. Neither of us believed that we would sit on the thrones of Kaphtu easily or quickly. Even if the Argives and their Kaphtui allies gave us no more trouble, Theseus would certainly have something to say about the choice of husband his daughter had made. We waited uneasily for the first ship to reach us from Athens after the ship had delivered Euphoros to answer to his master. Euphoros would almost certainly, we thought, make a big thing of our betrothal in order to distract attention from his own misdeeds.

But the ship arrived from Athens with nothing but routine messages from Theseus, and with no replacement for Euphoros as civil viceroy. The military viceroy was Phrasios, an Athenian who had been a Ground Dancer with Artimodorus's Dancers, the group that followed Brittomartis's fabled group. His loyalty to Theseus was unquestioned, but in the absence of any orders from him he made no difficulties about Akama taking Euphoros's powers. Once or twice he even consulted me on some minor matters concerned with coastal defense. I knew that at a word from Theseus he would try to kill or capture me, but for the moment he treated me almost as he would have treated Euphoros—indeed better, for I soon learned he had despised the blustering former viceroy. Phrasios had the Danaan attitude to women and preferred consulting me rather than Akama, but this merely amused her.

With the first ship back from the mainland, the second Dance of the season now took place. We kept almost entirely to the pattern of the Dance I had done with Ariadne disguised as Akama. We had time to practice it well, but not to make any innovations. Some of the Athenians were probably disappointed. The Athenian desire for new things has been a proverb ever since Erechthonios founded the city. But the mass of the crowd were Kaphtui and the Kaphtui like things to stay the same. The Kaphtui enthusiasts for the Dance say that only on seeing a group of Dancers do the same choreography for the second or third time can you appreciate the fine points of their performance.

We altered the order of Akama's last leap and mine, so that Akama could control the bull's last toss more precisely and the bull would have a lighter weight for his last toss. This worked very well and the second Dance was as great a success as the first. For me it had an even greater excitement, because I was performing with my beloved, and the little edge of danger that I had not felt performing with a goddess as Tauromath made my own performance better, I believe.

Akama had been a little nervous about her own first Dance and about what orders the ship from Athens would bring. With the Dance successfully over and no threats from an angry father on the ship from Athens, she swung over into complete euphoria. Every day she was as gay and excited as a child at a birthday feast. The old petulant look vanished from her face for good and she became more and more a popular favorite. I relaxed a little myself. If Theseus acted, he would have to move cautiously in the face of the popular enthusiasm for Akama.

But the next crisis did not come from any any action of Theseus's. I was crossing the Great Court one night after a late evening with Akama when I saw, standing in the doorway of the Room of the Path, a familiar figure, the figure I had known, ever since our last meeeting, I would have to face sooner or later. Apollo beckoned and I entered the Room of the Path, brushing past a guard who was as rigid and oblivious as a statue.

Pale-blue eyes met mine in a piercing stare. Whether or not the face and figure I saw were Apollo's real ones, I felt sure that I was seeing Apollo's real eyes. His voice, too, was an Olympian's voice with something in its timbre that sent a thrill through my body.

"Will you do me a service, Ducalion?" were his first words.

I wondered briefly what his reaction would be if refused, but one does not refuse an Olympian lightly. "If I can, my lord," I said as steadily as I could. "But what can a mortal do for one of the deathless gods?"

The answer was the one I had half expected, half feared; there is only one thing a mortal can do that a full-fledged Olympian cannot. "I want you to descend into the Dark Land," said the god's voice, calm and unmoved as if his statue in a temple had spoken, "and bring me news of what you find there."

The strange blue eyes bored into mine. "But you knew that, didn't you," he murmured. "Strange to find a mortal with some of my own power." His voice became brisker. "I'm glad you consent to help me, Duacalion. Believe me, the Shades of the Future in which you refuse to help me are unhappy ones for you. What I ask of you won't be easy, but the day will come when you will be glad you have done it."

I nodded, trying to keep my face impassive. That I would be glad someday was not to say that I might not be very sorry in the near future, but at least it was something. Apollo held out his hand with some familiar-looking wafers, like those Ariadne had given me the night before the Dance. "Take these," he said, "and throw them to the Guardian you will meet at the Iron Gates. You won't enter the Dark Land through this Path. I'm going to take you down the side slip to the path in the Cave at Amnisos. But the Guardian will be the same your friends told you of: a three-headed creature like a dog. Since Dion and the others were there, though, my uncle has built a stronghold on this hill in the Dark Land to guard the entrance better, and he's moved the Guardian to the other path. Nothing can get into or out of the Dark World on this path now, so you'll have to go in by way of the matching path in Amnisos."

He took me firmly by the elbow, and suddenly the Room of the Path twisted and blurred and we stood in the Holy Cave of Amnisos. His voice went on inexorably, "You'll have to make your way from this cave in the Dark Land to the hill where my uncle's stronghold stands. Tell those who guard the gate of the Hall that you are a messenger of mine. They'll take you to 'Dis—Adis, that is, Lord of the Dark World. Tell him that I saw what was done on the shores of Nysa and ask him what I am to tell the other Children of Kronos."

Apollo released my elbow and gestured to the pillar which joined the rocky ceiling to the floor of the Cave. "Go around that, keeping it on your left, until you reach the Dark Land. You will not be truly there until you cross water. You could make your way almost to the sronghold before you do that and avoid some dangers. But there are other dangers in walking on the Edges. Do what seems best to you at the time. Remember, you share my gift of seeing a little into the future. I will know when you return to this place, but nothing of what happens until then. I cannot promise that you will return safely, but if you do, you will have my gratitude and that is no small thing. Farewell."

I don't know if he touched me physically; I felt I had been pushed, and suddenly I found myself by the pillar, with the feeling that I was already one step outside of the world in which I had been born and lived. I felt a hot anger at Apollo, who was trying to manipulate me like a puppet, but this was overwhelmed by a rising excitement. I made myself stop and think, trying to feel the future possibilities as Apollo had told me I could do. Then I had an idea—or did I see a possibility glimmering ahead of me in my future?

I slowly and deliberately ate about half of the ambrosia cakes Apollo had given me. Then I started around the pillar, keeping it not on my left but on my right. The cave seemed to shift and change around me, and then I saw intoleerable brightness at the mouth of the cave. Reluctantly I turned my back on it and half knelt, half crouched on the floor of the cave, drawing deep breaths. My body began to tingle and I suddenly felt light and peaceful, bursting with energy. Even the brightness at the door of the cave was tolerable when I finally turned toward it. Half afraid, half fascinated, I moved closer to the entrance, keeping as much as I could to the darkest shadows.

What I could see was ordinary enough in one way: a little patch of beach and the sea beyond, very much what I would have seen from the Cave at Amnisos, for it is down the beach from the port. But I felt that I had never seen sand before, or sea, or the light on the sea. The world I had lived my life in seemed faded and dingy in memory: a tawdry copy of this glorious original.

I think I might have walked out that cave down onto the the sand like a man in a trance, but near the entrance some irregularity in the rock above let a little shaft of sunlight descend into the cave from the unseen sun above. I was holding my hands out in front of me as if I could grasp the scene before me and clutch it to my heart, and the shaft of light touched my right arm just above the wrist, just for an instant.

The pain was excruciating and as I leaped backwards, foolishly but instinctively grabbing at the arm, I saw that the skin was reddened and almost seared as if I had held it in a fire or it had been struck by a bolt of lightning. As I crouched, nursing my arm, the pain faded and the place where the sunbeam had touched me became white and only a little stiff, like an old wound. The scar formed a sort of irregular bar a little above my wrist, and though I felt that curious sense of peace and power coming back as the pain faded, I could hardly move the arm or the fingers of my right hand.

I could feel tears in my eyes, but somehow panic and worry left me along with the pain. I had been warned, sternly but mercifully. This land was not for mortals, and if I had stepped out into the full blaze of that sunlight I would have died, or gone back to my own world seared and scarred all over my body. But with the ambrosia I could not only live in the indirect light which shone into the cave, I could draw on it for energy, as I had drawn on the energy Ariadne had given me. Remembering another story of Aunt Brit's, I took one of my precious wafers of ambrosia and rubbed it over the hurt place on my arm. Gradually, feeling came back everywhere except in the scarred area itself, and I could move my arm and fingers again. The ambrosia seemed to liquefy as I rubbed it in, as a solidified cake of oil might do, and I rubbed the remnants of moisture over the other exposed parts of my body.

Then, my heart almost breaking for the land I could see but never enter, I turned to the pillar again and began walking around it, keeping it on my left, leaving the Bright Land behind, going to the lands of shadow and darkness.

Chapter Ten
ADIS

As I went back into the shadows, I found a curious reversal of my experience on the edge of the Bright Land. There I had seemed to myself a poor ghost in a solid and power-filled land, but as I walked the path I felt that I was solid and real and all about me was illusion. Somehow, I was aware when I was back in my own world, but I kept on circling the pillar, ready now to do Apollo's errand. Soon I felt rather than saw that I had come to the end of my journey. And as I stepped out into the dark cave, away from the pillar where the entrance must be, I could see that my body had a very faint golden glow. The scar on my arm shone with a paler color but a brighter glow.

As I approached the entrance, a dark form bulked up out of the shadows and a heart-stopping growl seemed to vibrate through the whole cave. Straining my eyes, I could see a nightmare form: three heads that it would be an insult to the canine race to call dogs' heads, a misshapen body and massive legs. Still feeling that curious sense of power and lightness, I slipped a single piece of ambrosia from my belt-pouch and held it so the creature could see what I had but not how much. I flipped the wafer so that it fell just under the creature's chest, so it had to lower its heads to search for it, then I vaulted over the creature's back as if it had been a bull and ran as hard as I could down the beach. A little brook was at my feet before I realized it, and I leaped it without thinking, realizing as I landed that one decision had made itself: I was now completely in the Dark Land, for better or worse.

Horrible sounds were coming from the cave. Somehow I knew that the creture's three heads were fighting over the ambrosia. At any rate, it was not pursuing me and I slowed to a walk, taking the direction that would have led me to N'sos in my own world. Aunt Brit's stories gave me some idea of what to expect, and I found everything just as she had described: the half-light, the lowering clouds, the somehow threatening quality of even the most innocent piece of vegetation. Despite the unvarying quality of the light, there seemed to be shadows moving on the edge of my vision, but whenever I looked hard at any place, thee shadows seemed to be still.

The setting was that of Aunt Brit's adventure, but I had neither Olympian powers nor Olympian companions. I ran toward the hills at a steady pace, trying to ignore the feeling that gliding shadows were keeping pace with me just out of my sight. The faint golden glow still clung to my body and I felt no fatigue and no real fear, although I wondered how I would have felt if I had not made my detour through the Bright Land. The shadows gradually seemed to be creeping up on each side of me, and a quick glance over my shoulder told me that I was being followed by a semicircle of dark, shifting shadow that partly concealed, partly revealed, the land behind me. I began to hear soft hissing sounds and occasionally a sound like a muffled groan or shriek.

My impulse was either to run faster or to stop and try to outface the shadowy followers, but I knew that either course would waste energy that I could not spare. I ran at a steady lope, followed by the shadows, which occasionally darted at me, always retreating. It was hard to tell whether that nightmare run was taking me a longer or shorter time than a similar journey in my own world would have, but presently I started down into the valley past the hill on which the Great House of N'sos stood in our world.

This hill was higher and rougher than the one in our world, which had been cut and carved to accommodate the palace of the Sea Kings. On it stood a jet black building, much smaller than the House of N'sos. Its walls leaned slightly inward and it had a grim, desolate look—definitely a fortress, and an embattled one, not a palace. So far as I could judge from the ground features that were the same in both worlds, it covered about the same ground as the northwest corner of the House; it must have been built chiefly to enclose and defend the entrance to the path which ended, in our world, in the Room of the Path in the palace.

I was following more or less the same path that the paved stone roadway from Amnisos to N'sos followed in our world, deviating occasionally to avoid obstacles which had been smoothed away centuries ago in my own world, when the road and the House itself had been renewed after the Year of Earthquakes. I wondered if the earth ever shook here, and if so what forces or beings made it shake. Not Posudi, the Earthshaker of our world, for of all the Children of Cronos only Adis, the oldest son, could come to this dark world, and he had paid the terrible price of exile

from the Bright Land for his lordship of this place. He
was, in fact, more jailer than ruler, having exiled
himself to keep ward and watch over the Titans who
had tried to destroy the Olympians and control the
world of mortals. I knew that some of these Old Ones,
cloaked in shadows, formed that dark semicircle which
inched toward me as I hesitated on the brink of the dry
ravine which separated me from the black fortress.

There was no causeway in this world, so I
scrambled down the side of the ravine and up the other
side. I saw nothing at the bottom but I felt stifled as I
got to the lowest point, and climbing up the farther side
was the hardest thing I had done since my entry into
Dark Land. Something which could not be seen lurked
in that place, and again I was sure that without my
detour into the Bright Land I would have been
captured or destroyed. That strength was ebbing now
and I clutched almost in despair at the coldy gleaming
Iron Gates before me in the fortress wall.

I had nothing to pound on them with until I picked
up a heavy stone from the ground near my foot and
hammered it against the place where the two gates met.
The sound seemed dead and tiny in the enormous
silence of that land, and there were no echoes from
within.

"I bear a message from Apollo, Son of Leto," I
cried hoarsely. "In the name of Zeus, Protector of
Travelers, and of the King above the Kings, let me
enter." The gates swung outward soundlessly,
grudgingly, just enough for me to slip between them.
As I leaped into the darkness within, they slammed
shut with a sonorous clang, and a moment later they

shook to the impact of heavy bodies hurling themselves against them from outside. The impact was like that of a ship, out of control, smashing a dock. I shuddered, wondering if those bodies belonged to the shadows that had followed me or to the invisible evil that lurked in the dry ravine.

As I stood in the dark, my breathing gradually eased and I felt comfortable for the first time since I had come to this dark country. There was a faint aromatic odor in the darkness that surrounded me, and just on the limit of my hearing faint traces of music seemed to sound. The pale glow that my flesh had held when I first came out of the path was gone, but there was still a gleam from the scar that the sunlight of the Bright Land had made on my arm.

Presently a faint gleam appeared ahead of me and as it brightened I saw that I was standing in a long corridor which seemed to be made of some gray stone, ashlar cut and marvelously fitted. The light was like torchight but steadier and more golden, and as it came toward me I could see that it came from the face of a young girl who was pacing slowly down the corridor toward me. She was dressed in the Kaphtui fashion and her bare arms and chest shone with the golden glow I had learned to associate with the Olympians, but her face was even brighter, so that it was hard to look directly into it. When I gave the salute which the Kaphtui give to goddesses and priestesses, shading my eyes with my hand carried to my brow, it was as much a natural reaction to the light from her face as it was a conventional gesture of respect.

"Blessings, P'dare," I said with what steadiness of voice I could muster.

She looked at me gravely. Her hair was as golden as my mother's but her face was that of an adolescent girl, lovely but willful and a bit petulant, yet at the same time a little shy and confused. It was a face that would not have surprised me on a mortal princess, especially in a Danaan land where women are protected and petted but have little independence. But it somehow took me aback to see that look on the face of an Olympian, which this girl very evidently was. Somehow I had thought that all Olympians would have that look of self-assurance and serenity that I was used to on the faces of Ariadne and Britomartis.

She looked at me a moment more and then raised her hand in a gesture that was curiously authoritative. Again I had a shock of recognition. "Blessings" is a common Kaphtui greeting, but she had taken it literally. I had asked for a blessing and she had given it, as one who had the power to give. Suddenly I had the same cold feeling of danger which I had felt on meeting Apollo. For all her girlish appearance, this Olympian girl had powers which I could only guess at.

She turned on her heel and started back the way she had come, evidently expecting me to follow her. My mind was working furiously as I started after her. The only Olympian who was supposed to live in this dark land was Adis, whom the Danaans call Hades. This Olympian maiden fit no tale or story I had heard, from Aunt Brit, from Ariadne, from any priest or priestess or minstrel. Something strange was going on here, and very clearly Apollo knew something of it, which explained this mission on which he had sent me.

We went up a stairway and down another corridor, finally brushing past a door-covering of some sort heavy cloth to enter a large room lit by what seemed to be ordinary firelight. There was a circular hearth in the center of the rom like those in the mainland Danaan palaces and a cheerful fire crackled on it, the smoke going up into the shadowy heights of the room. Aunt Brit had told me of the austerity of most Olympian dwellings, but this room was as richly decorated as a Kaphtui palace room: there were wall paintings, the gleam of gold and ivory inlay on the carven furniture and the cloth hangings at the doors were richly embroidered. Sitting in a high-backed wooden chair near the hearth was a bearded man, and the golden haired girl slipped into a similar chair at his side.

She fixed her eyes on me, but for the moment I had no eyes for her; my gaze was fixed on her companion. The pale face, the intensely blue-black hair, the look of stern grandeur—this could only be Adis, son of Cronos, brother of Zeus and Posudi. I gave him the salute I would have given a ruler or a sea captain: clenched fist carried to the forehead, thumb in.

"I am on an errand from Apollo, the Son of Leto, my lord," I said. "He asked me to give you this message. He saw what was done on the plain of Nysa. He wishes to know what it is your will that he do."

Those intensely dark eyes were boring into mine and I was almost, but not quite, oblivious to the girl beside him. But I heard her draw in her breath and out of the corner of my eye I saw her turn to Adis, her hand clutching his arm. Whatever the relationship between these two, my curious message from Apollo had frightened the girl and in her fright she instinctively turned to Adis for support. He took his eyes from mine and touched her hand gently with his own, smiling gravely at her. Then he turned to me again, but the first thing he said was not a reply to my words.

"You are not an Olympian, young man," came the deep calm voice that sent a shiver down my spine. "Despite my long absence from the High World I am sure of that. Are you the son of one of my brothers or nephews?"

I shook my head. "No, my lord. My name is Akademus, called Ducalion. My mother is Alceme, daughter of Akademus of the House of Erechthonius, and my father was N'suto, son of M'nos the Dark and of Riamare, Daughter of Kariatu. Perhaps the blood of Posudi and Hephaestos runs in my veins, but very thinly."

That grave smile touched the corners of his mouth and he said in his deep voice, "Perhaps not so thinly. Very few mortals could have made the journey from the Cave to this house. My nephew chose his messenger wisely. As to his message..." The voice grew sterner and deeper. "Tell him that what he knows is known to my brother and that he would do well to keep out of the affair. He can do nothing to help and perhaps much to harm. I make no threats and no promises, but Apollo would do well to heed my words." His voice was calm and uninflected, but I thought that even Apollo, had he stood where I was standing, would have been chilled by those words, as I was even though I was only a messenger.

Adis perhaps saw the strain on my face and he smiled at me again, this time with genuine kindness. "My nephew will no doubt go his own way, whatever I say; that is not your responsibility, lad. I would willingly offer you some refreshment but it would be poor hospitality—perhaps you know that?"

I nodded with a little internal shudder. Eating anything from this place would tie me to it and pull me back sooner or later to this dark land. "Yes, lord," I replied. "Aunt Brit—Britomartis that is—told me a little about her visit to this land with Ariadne and Dion. All three of them are friends of my family…" I went on uncertainly for I had definitely disturbed their Olympian calm. The girl's hand went to her mouth and she bit at her knuckles in a curiously childish gesture. Adis rose to his feet, his heavy robe swirling about him with the suddenness of his motion.

"The Blessed Three," he exclaimed. "I and all the Olympians owe them more than we can repay. If you are a friend of theirs you are thrice welcome." Again there was a faint smile. "More welcome than you were as Apollo's messenger, though I did not blame you for his meddling. I wish more than ever I could give you proper hospitality."

Moved by a sudden impulse, I pulled the remaining ambrosia from my belt pouch. "Would you honor me by sharing this with me, my lord and lady?"

He took it into his hands almost reverently. "Little of this reaches us from the Bright Land," he said softly. "The gift is as welcome as the chance to share it with you."

He broke the wafer and shared it with us. Simple as the action was, I have never in court or temple seen a ceremony so impressive. It was the ceremonial sharing of food between guest and host, but it was also in some way a sharing of ourselves with each other.

The girl spoke now for the first time in a soft, husky voice. "Is it spring still in the world of mortals?" she asked wistfully.

"High summer, my lady," I said gently, and then, moved by some impulse to make the world outside of this dark land less attractive, I said, "A bad summer for the land, lady. The crops have had a hard time since the Year of the Great Wave. The dust from the fire mountain keeps falling and choking out the young plants."

Her face was suddenly tragic as she looked into my eyes. I saw that her eyes were a curious shade of blue, almost violet. "It may be worse for the land when my mother learns what has happened, with or without 'Pollo's meddling."

Adis turned toward her with a curiously protective gesture, as if he were shielding her from something. "Do you regret, now, what has happened?" he asked softly.

She shook her head. "No, oh no," she said clutching his hand in hers, and I realized that whatever else these two were, they were lovers. "I miss the sun and the growing things, but my place is here with you. My mother, though, will never accept that. There will be trouble—terrible trouble for men and gods—before this is resolved."

Chapter Eleven
THE STOLEN GODDESS

I looked at the two of them, puzzled and uneasy, but Adis's dark eyes caught mine again. "There is a bond between us now," he said, "but I will not burden you with the quarrels of the Olympians. Such is my kingdom that the best hospitality I can give you is to see you safely out of it, but we will not forget you." He brooded for a moment, then said, half to himself, "You were in greater danger than you know, young man. You are of the blood of M'nos, whom mortals remember as the Dark. And he is in this land, imprisoned along with the Old Ones whom he tried to make his allies. It is not safe for you to leave this House to reach the path you came by. Blood calls to blood and he might be able to use you in some way against your will. There is no help for it, I will have to reopen the path I sealed when I built this place."

When he had said, "It is not safe for you to House," my heart had almost stopped at the thought that I might be trapped here; now my heart gave a great bound. To be able to get back to my own world without traversing that deadly landscape again and meeting the fearful guardian of the path was more than I had dreamed of hoping.

Adis gestured to me, and with the blonde girl between us we went ou the door. The room seemed cozy and normal while we were in it, but as I glanced behind me before leaving it, I noticed that the logs of which the fire was made burned brightly with no apparent dimunition or change and the smoke still ascended straight and still, despite the stir made by our movements; that was no ordinary log fire.

We went down several dark corridors and then through a series of lighted rooms, lit this time not with firelight but with a golden glow like the sun of the Bright Land, coming from what seemed to be alabaster globes and with plants and flowers growing in pots and stone chests filled with dirt. The plants grew luxuriously enough and the flowers were lovely. There was even a little fountain playing, with moss in its crevices. But this indoor place with its unwavering light was a poor substitute for open sky and natural growth. I remembered the little valley where Akama and I had picnicked, contrasting it in my mind with this artificial "outdoors."

At last we came to a curious room lit by the same alabaster globes, whose only furnishing was a massive block of stone flanked by what seemed to be immense carved gryphons. Then I drew in a breath so hard it was painful, as I realized that living eyes were looking at me from the apparent carvings. That these were living creatures was confirmed in a moment as Adis stepped forward and spoke to them.

"What was closed must be opened," he said solemnly, "to repay old debts. This youth is a friend of Britomartis, at whose request you came to help me in my viigil. He is of the blood of M'nos and I do not dare let him return the way he came."

A curiously high, remote voice came, a single voice but somehow seeming to come from both gryphons. "At your word, lord, and for the sake of the Golden Lady, it shall be done."

Suddenly the face of the stone was no longer blank but had massive iron gates in it. Iron again! I questioned Adis hesitantly. "When Britomartis and the others were here they saw iron gates as they came out of the Path…"

Adis nodded. "They are at every place where the Old Ones might seek to enter a path or a stronghold of mine. The iron is real iron, forged by Hephaestos. It will be years before you mortals can forge even small pieces of it."

I nodded. It was every metalworker's dream to work iron, but it was either too tough to work at all or shattered like a fine clay pot when it was heated and tempered.

Adis continued, "The Old Ones have a special difficulty with iron, and with running water. They can overcome either one if they have their full power, but it drains their strength. And they have little strength to waste now."

I touched the doors wonderingly. They were formed of interlaced bars, woven together as tightly as a basket is woven. To forge such a massive thing in bronze would be beyond the power of any craftsman, except perhaps the legendary Daedalus, and forged in iron they were a wonder indeed.

Now Adis was speaking again. "Go with my blessings, Akademus, called Ducalion. Someday you or yours may want something from me and if it is in my power to give it, I will give it gladly. Your youth and courage have lightened our dark house for a little while." He lifted his hand in blessing and stepped back.

119

The blonde girl stepped forward impulsively and said, "Greet Britomartis for me, if you see her. My name is Persephone; she knows me. Tell her…" She paused and bit her lip.

"I will tell her, lady, that you are content to stay with your lord," I said gently.

She smiled brilliantly, her true beauty shining forth. "Yes, tell her that," she said almost gaily. "Tell her, and anyone else who will listen." Her head lifted proudly, defying I know not whom or what.

The iron gates swung open silently on a shadowy corridor whose walls were curiously misty, and with a deep breath I stepped over the threshold. As I turned to speak words of thanks and farewell, I had my last sight of Adis and Persephone. She was leaning against him, her eyes wistful, as I left them for a world of light and freedom. His arm was around her in that curiously protective way and his pale face was somber. Despite their gloomy surroundings, they seemed to find happiness in each other, and I thought of some words of Aphea's that Ariadne was fond of repeating: "It's better to suffer anything with the one you love rather than be separated."

Suddenly I thought of Akama and a desire to be with her swept over me. I strode down the shadowy corridor, beginning to worry about how long I had been away. In Aunt Brit's stories sometimes she had been in the Bright Land only a short time and found on her return that a much longer time had passed in the world of mortals. Did this apply to the Dark World, too? My adventures had only seemed to take a few hours, but could I have been missing from my own world for days? What would Akama think if I had?

As on my journey in the other direction, something told me when I approached our own world on the shadowy Path. Gradually I saw a faint image of the Room of the Path looming up before me and getting more solid as I got closer to it. Fighting the impulse to pass my own world and return to the fatal beauty of the Bright Land, I moved toward the image of the Room of the Path, centrating on my longing for Akama. Just as I felt solid stone under my feet instead of the curiously yielding surface of the path, something rushed toward me, somehow seeming to come from the right, though all that was there was the shadowy wall of the path. For a second, I had the image of a gold-glowing face, noble but stern, which bore a faint resemblance to the disguised face Apollo had shown me.

The face and a faint suggestion of a lightly clad, gold-glowing body seemed to rush not so much past me as through me. My head whirled, and then all of a sudden I was standing at the top of the steps which came up from the Sacred Pit in the Room of the Path. Although I seemed to have come up those steps, I knew without looking that the fine sand scattered in the bottom of the pit would show no sign of footsteps. Standing in the middle of the room was Apollo, disguised again as a mortal. Still worrying about how long I had been gone, I glanced out the door into the Great Courtyard. It was dark and deserted; it must be late at night, but was it the same night here as when I had left?

Apollo guessed or perhaps saw my thought. "You have been gone only a few moments by the time of this world," he said. "It was more difficult than it should have been to bring you back near the time you left. Somewhere you acquired a great deal of energy." I volunteered no information. He had sent me on a mission from which I might easily never have returned, and I felt I owed him no explanations. Whether it was in response to this thought or not, Apollo went on. "I was sure you would come back. The futures in which you did not were very dim. How you did it is your affair, but you must have found favor with my uncle, to be coming back by this path. I thought he had sealed it forever. Tell me all you saw and heard. You will not find me ungrateful."

I gave him Adis's answer to his question and, in response to some probing questions, told him something of my conclusions about Persephone's relationship with Adis. Then I burst out, "Tell me what all this about. You owe me that much."

His face became a little sterner at my bluntness, but his words were courteous enough. "That much and a great deal more. What you have told me is something I could have learned in no other way. Persephone showed her feelings before you because you are a mortal, not an Olympian."

I could fill in the implications for myself. An Olympian would not guard herself before a mortal any more than a mortal princess would bother to dissemble before a slave or a pet.

Apollo paused as if to marshall his thoughts and then went on. "Persephone is the daughter of my father's sister, Demeter. My uncle has been fond of her since she was a child. She loves growing things and often comes to your world to enjoy the changes of seasons and weather. Adis can't return to Olympus but he can come to this world if he wishes, and he has been meeting her on these visits. She became fond of him, first in a childish way, then more deeply. Finally Adis asked my father for his approval of the marriage. They both knew that Demeter would never give her consent. She dotes on her daughter and would never agree to be parted from her. So, with my father's permission, Adis lured Persephone away from her companions on one of her visits to this world and took her down to the Dark World. I saw it happen, more or less by accident. Persephone acted as if she were surprised and shocked, but I don't think she was really all that reluctant. She's young enough to find it romantic to be carried off by a lover. What you saw confirms that; you say that she and Adis seem to be happy with each other."

His face took on a brooding look and he spoke half to himself. "Demeter is the problem. She's acting like a mad creature, rushing about looking for her daughter. She's powerful, very powerful, and no one can influence her. Perhaps Hestia could, but she never interferes And Demeter knows already that her daughter has been stolen away somehow. Ekata got wind of something and passed it on to Demeter, currying favor. I don't trust Ekata, even though she's supposed to be a friend of the Olympians…"

I felt a sort of uneasy thrill. Ekata, whom the Danaans call Hecate, was one of the Old Ones, a cousin of Ria whose mating with Cronos had produced

Zeus and his brothers and sisters. I had heard Aunt Brit refer to her in the same distrustful way. She was not one of Those Below, the rebel Old Ones whose jailer was Adis, but she was worshiped with strange rites and sacrifices. He priestesses were feared and called "witch" behind their backs. Hers was a name I would rather not have heard in connection with this affair.

I was sure I had thought that rather than saying it aloud, but Apollo's next remark seemed to be a response. "You know a great deal about the Olympians and Old Ones, don't you, my young friend? Perhaps more than is safe for a mortal. You will speak to no one of these things, if you are wise. And I perhaps would be wise to say nothing of what you have told me. But all the futures I can see are dark. Telling Demeter what I know may be the best choice of all…" His eyes looked into mine, "Some things in your future I can see, Akademus. If things go as I see them now I will not be able to help you in your greatest need, but there will be a great thing which you will ask of me and which I will be able to grant. Rest now. The trouble I can see will not come for awhile."

With these words of dubious cheer he vanished, and suddenly weariness struck me like a blow. Foggily remembering that he had told me that I had been gone from my own world only a short time, I staggered to my room and collapsed on the bed, wearier even than I had been the night before my first Dance. For a few minutes whirling thoughts kept me awake, but soon I fell into sleep, restless sleep at first filled with dreams of what I had experienced, then deep sleep into which I plunged as a sponge diver plunges into the depths.

I awoke with late-afternoon sun in my eyes to find an unfamiliar woman's face bending over mine. As I blinked the sleep from my eyes, I recognized her as a Healer who was one of Akama's ladies.

"They couldn't wake you this morning, my lord," she said. "My lady gave orders to let you sleep, but had me come to watch by your side. I told her when she came at noon it was weariness, not sickness, and I see I was right. I will go now, and tell her you are awake."

I stretched, swung my legs over the side of the bed and sat up. "Tell her I'll be with her as soon as I can wash and change my kilt," I said.

The Healer nodded and left the room with the curious gliding walk affected by many of the priestesses. Like many Healers, she was a priestess of Artemis, and I wondered what she would have said if I had told her that had been running errands for her goddess's brother.

As soon as I could make myself reasonably presentable, I went straight to Akama. She was occupying herself with palace business but she looked distracted ane worried. When I appeared at the door she dismissed the stewards she had been talking to and flew into my arms. The stewards smiled to each other as they left, but they were indulgent smiles and not mocking ones. Without having done much to deserve it, Akama and I were great favorites with everyone in the palace.

We sat together on a window seat, with arms around each other, while I told her about my adventures of the night before. I tried to minimize the dangers, but she clutched me very tightly as my story unfolded, and traced the scar on my arm with a gentle finger. It already looked healthy and well healed, like a scar years old, but I was aware of a sort of tingle in it; indeed, I am sometimes aware of it still.

When my story was finished, though, her first words were not of me, or of Apollo's predictions, but of Persephone. "It's all very well for Apollo to say that she's fond of Adis and for Zeus to give her away in marriage, but no one seems to have consulted the girl herself. Adis just swooped her up and took her down to that awful place. And you say she loves the weather and growing things. My sympathies are with her and her mother. She must be frantic, not knowing what's happened to her daughter."

I nodded. "You're right, of course. The male Olympians all have the Danaan attitude to women, except for Dion. They wouldn't think of doing anything as sensible as consulting the girl herself. But however it's started, she's in love with Adis now and content to be there with him. And if she's really a full Olympian, she can't go back to Olympus now. Britomartis and Ariadne and Dion could go to the Dark Land and return because they're half mortal. But shes not there against her will and even if she were we couldn't help her."

She smiled at me affectionately. "I wasn't thinking of asking you to go and rescue her. My indignation doesn't extend to risking you. I thought more of telling Ariadne, if we could reach her. I guess we had probably better keep out of the affairs of the Olympians. I'm just grateful to have you back, and grateful that you are what you are."

I kissed her hands gently and raised them to my forehead as I had the first day we met. I knew what she was thinking. I had always treated her as a person in her own right, even apart from my respect for her as a princess and as Mistress of the Dance. But no one raised by my mother and grandmother could take women lightly, even apart from the influence of Aunt Brit, Ariadne and Dion. Dion treated women with more respect than men, simply because he felt they deserved it more. His frightening side was usually shown to men.

At the thought of Dion's sometimes terrifying aspect, my thought grew somber again. I held Akama tight and spoke my thought. "We can leave the Olympians alone, my love; indeed we have little choice. But will they leave us alone?"

Chapter Twelve
TWO BLOWS

Despite Apollo's dark hints, the days that followed were peaceful. Since the Argive raids in the Year of the Great Wave and after, the other palaces had not been rebuilt and the Dance no longer went on tour to the palaces in other parts of Kaphtu, but there were regular performances at N'sos, building up to the final Dance of the season. Akama and I looked forward to this final Dance because it would mark the real beginning of our marriage. Even aside from the old stories about a female Tauromath losing her power if she lost her virginity, no one could carry on a normal married life while serving as Tauromath and Mistress of the Dance. Akama was longer bone weary from practice as she had been in the first days, but she needed every bit of concentration and energy to manage her bull and her Dancers. When you added to this the administrative duties that had fallen on her shoulders since Euphoros had left Kanhtu, she had enough to handle without becoming a bride, too.

We both realized this and agreed on it, but that did not make it any easier for us to wait. So we flung ourselves into preparations for our last Dance, trying to make it a fitting finale to our careers as Dancers. It is still talked of in Kaphtu, though perhaps not with the same awe as the legendary last Dance of Aunt Brit's troupe. I wished she or my mother could have seen it, for we performed as we never had before, inspired by our love for each other and by the enthusiasm of the crowds.

We had agreed to meet at the little valley after the Dance. A sort of shyness kept us from going there together and we had no thought of danger, for we had often visited the valley for relaxation during that summer. Akama's happy experience with the Wild Ones in the valley had removed the unpleasant associations of her injury there, and something of the presence of the Wild Ones seemed to linger there. If we could have reached the valley, I think we would have been spared a great deal of suffering, but perhaps also we would have missed some things of great value.

What intercepted me on my way to the valley did not seem very formidable at first. As I passed through the fields on my way there, I saw the bent figure of what appeared to be an old woman, wrapped in a dark cloak and bearing two long torches, burning smokily in the bright afternoon sunlight. If this was some ceremony of mourning or prayer it was one unfamiliar to me, and having other things on my mind, I would have passed the woman with a gesture of respect, but I found my arm grasped with unexpectedly powerful fingers and I looked into a strange face with wild eyes from which something like madness peered. With a sinking of my heart, I realized that the face was that of no mortal woman, and that it bore a faint but definite resemblance to that of my hostess in the Dark Land, Persephone.

Her words soon confirmed this. "You know, you know something," she said in a deep voice which sent a shiver up my spine. "Hecate says so, and she knows, she finds out things for me. Look at me, boy." Her glittering eyes seeemed to bore into mine and chaotic memories of my trip to the Dark Land rushed through my mind. Somehow I was sure she was sorting through my memories as I might sort through a bale of goods. She pushed me away and her lip curled in contempt.

"Fool," she said, "Adis tricked you, tricked you as he tricked my daughter. She can't be happy with him, happy in that place." She rocked back and forth clutching herself as if in agony. "She was conceived in these fields, the thrice-plowed fields, and now she lies down in darkness. Woe to the fields! Woe to you and all mortals until my daughter returns to me!" She bent down and with a swoop like a hawk's her hand scooped up earth and scattered it to the wind. With horror, I saw that where the fragments of earth landed the growing things withered and died, and the destruction spread from plant as fast as a man could walk. Without another word she stalked off, swinging her torches and keening, "Woe, woe."

I looked after her, my head whirling and my happiness shattered. What right had the Olympians to involve us in their quarrels? If this withering spread from field to field there would be starving people in this land that I already thought of as mine. The sea could feed us for awhile and if it was only the cultivated fields that suffered, perhaps the beasts would survive. But bread was the staple of every poor man's diet; what would we do for bread?

I started for the valley again. I was in no mood, now, for honeymooning, but I wanted Akama, wanted her counsel and comfort. A hoarse cry from behind me made me wheel around. A man was staggering toward me from the direction of the palace, bent over, with one hand clutched to his shoulder. As he came closer, I saw it was S'tono and I ran to his aid. He collapsed into my arms and I could see that he had a deep stab in his shoulder and nasty cuts on his arms and hands and head. I tried to wipe the blood from his face but he waved me aside with a feeble hand.

"Akama," he croaked, "they have Akama."

I stopped my futile attempt to stanch the blod and gripped his shoulders. "Who?" I rapped out in a voice I didn't recognize as my own.

"Theseus, her father," he gasped and I bent my head closer to hear his feeble voice. "Appeared from nowhere with a group of men. Some of them looked...like sailors. Snatched her up...beat off those who tried to stop...went...toward...coast." Having got out the essentials he let go at last and lapsed into merciful unconsciousness.

I laid him gently back on the ground and looked down at his face for a moment, my thoughts frozen. Then somehow I found strength—I think I became a man there in that dusty field. I had been a boy before, playing at adventures. My mind began to work again. Theseus must know that Akama and I were too popular to be separated by a mere command or by any measure short of an armed invasion from Athens. His answer had been this sudden raid with, very likely, only one ship. That would be his style, alone with only a shipful of fellow daredevils to snatch his daughter from her throne.

Where would his ship be? Not at Ammsos—too public. One of Aunt Brit's stories flashed into my mind. The little cove where his ship had been hidden when he fled from Kaphtu with Ariadne! He might have used it again, probably had, for he had no way of knowing that anyone now alive in Kaphtu knew of his previous use of it.

I set off at a steady run across the fields, grudging the few moments it took me to send the first peasant woman I found in the fields back to help S'tono. I headed for the road from N'sos to Amnisos, hating the extra distance, but knowing I could make better time on the road than attempting a shortcut over fields and hills. When I reached the road I ran down it toward the sea. At the first guard post I rapped out orders. Two guards followed me and the third went at a run for the nearest hill post. After that I simply ran full tilt for Aninisos, letting the guards pass on my orders as we passed each post. The orders were simply to get every armed man to the harbor as soon as possible. I needed men and ships now; everything else could wait.

At the harbor I went straight to the *Purple Oar,* the premier ship of the Kaphtui fleet. Seamen were sent running for whatever oarsmen could be found, no matter what ship they belonged to, and for any officers that could be summoned at short notice. Luckily, the captain of the Purple Oar lived near the harbor and just as we had a full complement of oarsmen and enough road and harbor guards to give us a fighting force, he jumped aboard, pushing aside the captain of a lesser ship who had been about to take us out to sea. The other captain saluted and ran for his own ship, gathering oarsmen from those who stood on the dock begging to be allowed aboard the ship I was in. As we moved out of the harbor under oars, sailing masters from two different ships were making sure that our sail was ready to set. Our captain told the soldiers where to find stored weapons aboard, then turned to me.

I explained my guess as to where Theseus's ship had been hidden and he nodded grimly and gave orders to the steersman.

"They'll want to slip away without being seen much from shore and get clear of established shipping routes as soon as possible," he said. "That gives them a limited number of courses to steer, and on this course we'll intercept any route they can take. The sailing master will give us the sail as soon as it will do any good." His eyes raked the seamen who were not actually at the oars. "Here, you boy, up the mast and keep an eye out for any ship, but especially any one that looks Danaan."

I called as the boy swarmed up the mast, "It may have black sails."

For the moment there was nothing more to do. I looked behind us, and two more ships were alredy out of the harbor, loaded but not overloaded with armed men. Not all of them were soldiers. Somebody with sense had opened arms stores in the harbor and armed porters and dock officials. On the second ship I could see one of the wealthiest merchants in Amnisos, captaining one of his own ships. All this on a few orders from a man who had not set foot in Kaphtu at the beginning of this year.

I looked into the captain's eyes. "The man we're hunting is Theseus," I said, "rightful king of Kaphtu."

He shook his head slowly. "He hasn't set foot in Kaphtu in over eight years," he said bitterly. "By

Kaphtui law that's an abdication, unless he's at sea in a Kaphtui ship. He held the throne only by his marriage to the daughter of the last M'nos. By interfering with your marriage to his daughter, he's spitting on the very law by which he held the throne himself."

I was silent for a moment, considering. "The Athenian alliance protects Kaphtu from the Argives," I said, feeling a strange unreality in debating such matters as I strained every nerve toward the unseen ship which held Akama.

The captain shook his head stubbornly. "He's used violence to the Holy One of Ria," he said. "No Kaphtui will follow him now, no matter what the consequences. You are M'nos now, my lord. It is fitting that you be told that on the deck of the first ship of your fleet. Take the captain's chair and I'll give you my oath on the Sacred Oar itself, it's on board."

I shook my head, thinking it no time for ceremonies, but his horny seaman's hand pressed me down into the chair. "If it comes to a fight, my lord, it might save some of the men from wavering," he murmured.

I nodded assent then. My worry about whether I could trust these men to follow me if Theseus asserted his authority as ruler of Kaphtu was the reason I had raised the matter with the captain in the first place. They could see what was happening from the nearer ships and when the captain, after taking the oath, gave me the salute given only to a captain on his own ship or to M'nos himself, the men rested on their oars for a moment and gave a ragged cheer, then dug in again with renewed energy.

The wind was still not serving the sail and we had just changed oarsmen when the lookout up the mast cried out, "A ship with a black sail furled on its yard. Over toward Dia."

I was up the mast myself in a moment as high as I could climb it and located the ship, trying to hide its outline against the rocky shores of the little island. My heart was pounding as we closed the distance, the fresh oarsmen fairly lifting the ship out of the water. I saw the gleam of bronze on the deck and knew that we had found Theseus; a ship of armed men with a black sail could only be his.

It was soon obvious that the black-sailed ship could not escape, and it soon hove to, waiting our approach. My nerves were stretched as taut as the bowstrings of the archers on deck. Surely Theseus would not surrender tamely. If there was a fight, what might happen to Akama? But the men in the ship were not standing to arms, and as we drew closer I could see Akama in a bedraggled festival gown standing on the deck next to a dark -haired man with touches of gray in his hair and an air of command.

I strained my eyes to see Theseus, the almost legendary warrior and adventurer who was the father of my Akama. As we came within bowshot, he reached to his side almost casually and drew his sword. He set the point against Akamaís side, just below her left breast and looked into my face. At my gesture, the captain gave low-voiced orders to the oarsmen to rest on their oars. The two ships drifted slowly closer, the wind, which was against us, gradually slowing our ship.

"Unless my ship goes free, *with* the girl, she dies," came Theseus's voice, calm and almost conversational. We were close enough to see his eyes; there was madness lurking in them.

My only hope was to taunt him into a fight. I tried to make my voice lightly mocking as I said, "Hiding behind a woman's skirts, *hero* of Athens? Come fight like a man."

I laid my hand on my own sword, which someone had strapped around me when the ships were closing. He would probably kill me, of course—he was the victor in a thousand battles—but what other hope did I have of saving Akama?

Almost gently he took that hope away. "I don't want your life, boy." He smiled mirthlessly.

"Just my daughter. I have a use for her."

When you are a real hero you can afford to refuse to fight an untried youth, I thought miserably, and men will call it mercy, not cowardice. I would not taunt Theseus into a fight.

I looked into Akama's eyes, the narrow corridor of water that separated us seeming to stretch out to a sundering sea. "I'll come for you my love," I said. "To Athens or to the Halls of Adis."

She looked back at me with a little smile that tore at my heart. "I know you will, my husband," she said.

Theseus's nostrils flared, then he laughed bitterly. "Get her off the Hill of Athens, boy, and you can have her with my blessing," he jeered. With reason: the High-city of the Hill of Athens is the most impregnable fortress in any Danaan land. Then a thought he didn't like struck Theseus. "But no help from your cursed Olympian friends, boy, or I'll…"

I could see the sword tip drawing blood from the skin below Akama's bare breast. "Agreed," I said.

"Swear by the River of Death," he demanded, and I gave him the oath that even the Olympians fear to break.

He laughed shortly and sheathed his sword. "Then I look forward to welcoming you to Athens," he jeered. "But watch your coasts. I've told the Argives that my protection is removed from Kaphtu." Then to his captain, "Let's get under way. Direct to Athens. We won't be followed."

I stood watching as the Athenian ship moved off, until I could no longer see Akama. Then I turned to the captain. "Back to Amnisos. When we get there I must go up to the palace for a short time. When I get back I want the fastest ship in the harbor that isn't recognizably a Kaphtui ship, with a crew of men who can pass as Danaans. I want a good captain and crew. We're going to reach Athens before Theseus does."

The captain grinned wolfishly. "You have me."

I shook my head. "You have a harder task, captain. You're going to be regent of Kaphtu until I return. I don't even know your name, I'm afraid."

Pride struggled in his face with genuine disappointment as he said, "I'll not fail you, my lord. My name is M'suno, 'the Sea King's man.' May it be a good omen."

I had to sit like a statue in the captain's chair on our way home. No one but the captain was close enough to see the tears in my eyes. In the litter they called for me at the dockside to take me to N'sos. I tried to keep my mind blank, but I kept wanting to throw up, and not being able to manage it, I felt cold and my skin was clammy. At the palace word had somehow gone before me; I never knew how swiftly rumor could fly until that day. People stepped aside with sorrowful respect as I went straight to the Room of the Path. I leaned against a pillar and groaned aloud, then called on Apollo with every power I could summon.

Instantly he was there. I saw his true face now and the shock of that somehow steadied me. He looked intently into my eyes.

"Theseus extracted some sort of promise from you, so that I can't help you over the stealing of your wife," he said. It was not a question, but I nodded my head. His face was brooding. "I saw that, Akademus, but it couldn't be stopped without worse things happening later on. Do you know what you do want me to do?"

I drew a deep breath. "Theseus has thrown Kaphtu to the Argive wolves. I don't know why, but I can't leave the country defenseless, even to rescue Akama. Can you guard it?"

He nodded grimly and the smile he gave reminded me of Captain M'suno's wolfish grin. "Anyone who tried to land on the coasts of Kaphtu with hostile intent will be very, very sorry, I assure you, my young friend," he said. The brooding look returned. "Rescue your Akama," he said. "You can do it. I wish it were as possible to get Persephone back from Adis. Demeter is going mad and doing terrible things. I must go. Farewell."

He was gone. I had a reminder if I needed one of what I needed to do next. I called the chief steward, warned him of famine to come and gave him authority to ration grain. "Don't even waste seed trying to plant until the fields are healthy again," I said. "Keep seed grain at any cost, but distribute grain from the palace stores to keep people from starving. We can buy grain from Egypt next year, perhaps, and if worse comes to worst the sea will keep us alive."

He shook his head forebodingly. "There are so many people, lord. Too many perhaps. But we will do what we can. Bring your lady back to us, lord, and we can survive anything, for this land without an Ariadne will no longer be Kaphtu."

I set out for the harbor then and the waiting ship. His words echoed in my heart and I added others of my own to them. Now that I had known and loved her, I without Akama would no longer be myself. By my own vow I could not call on Britomartis or Ariadne for help. But I must rescue Akama or die in the attempt.

Chapter Thirteen
THE HILL

Astoundingly few days later we were dropping anchor near Piraeus, a little fishing village down the coast from Phaleron, the port of Athens. Even despite my gnawing worry about Akama, my mind still worked in accustomed ways, and I remember thinking that with a little work the harbor at Piraeus could be made a better port for Athens than Phaleron would ever be. I looked over my landing party with foreboding. They were a strangely assorted crew. So swiftly had word of Akamaís kidnapping spread, that they even included two of the men who had conspired against Akama and me. They had been waiting at the ship to beg me on their knees to take them so that they could make reparation for their previous deeds. Since I knew that they were already enemies of Theseus, I accepted them. My fear was that men who looked Danaan enough to serve my plans might have too many Danaan sympathies.

We were dressed in an assortment of Danaan garments—whatever had been available in Amnisos when we left. Some garments had literally been snatched from the backs of men in the dock area, so great was our hurry to get under way. I had given the best garments to those who seemed best able to maintain the part of Danaan noblemen. The rest of us were dressed as servants or retainers. Luckily, a country nobleman coming from his estates to Athens would have armed retainers with him, so we were able to carry our swords openly.

140

My own features were too markedly Kaphtui to pass as any kind of Danaan. Fortunately, there had been a fashion for Kaphtui stewards among the wealthier nobles, and I was playing the part of such a steward. This enabled me to give orders openly to the other "servants" while pretending to take them from the "nobleman" and his "friends." Ironically enough, the one best fitted to play the part of the supposed chief nobleman was Hyperes, one of the two men who had been banished to their estates for their part in the plot against Akama. He was the younger son of a nobleman whose estates were in the remoter parts of Attika, and he had gone to Kaphtu to improve his fortunes. His family, like many of the old Attikan nobility, resented Theseus's accession to the throne of Aegeus, and so Hyperes had been easily drawn into the plot against the rule of Theseus in Kaphtu. Of course, he also had in mind the wealth and power a successful rebellion might bring to the rebels. He claimed to have been impressed by Akama's merciful treatment of the more innocent rebels and swore that he would give his life to rescue her.

When he had said that, I felt a sudden dark foreboding that he and many of this crew of volunteers might do just that, give their lives in this desperate rescue attempt. My foresight, if indeed I had such a power, had not warned me of the kidnapping of Akama or the threat to Kaphtu, but it is said that even a true prophet cannot forsee his own fate or those of people too closely connected with him. Nor can a mortal with prophetic gifts forsee what the gods will do. It seemed to me that my supposed gift of foresight was worse than useless, since it could not fortell the two worst blows I had suffered in my life and was good only to give me useless forebodings about the fate of my crew. Useless, for I knew that if I were sure that all of them would die in rescuing Akama I would still try to rescue her.

The Attikan countryside was peaceful since the accesion of Theseus, who had put down robbery and feuding among the nobles with a strong hand. But to keep the peace there were roving patrols of Athenian troops, often mercenary soldiers under an Athenian commander, since mercenaries would be impartial in local quarrels. Our elaborate charade was due to our fear that we would be stopped and questioned by such a patrol.

At first our luck held. We aroused no curiosity in Piraeus, for the overflow of ships from Phaleron were beginning to use the natural harbor there and the fishermen were used to strange vessels. Nor did we face any challenges on our way to Athens. Coming from any direction but from the sea our lack of horses and chariots would have caused comment, for Danaans are all horse-mad. But no one can carry horses and chariots in a ship and no one but a king can arrange to be met on his arrival, for landfalls are too uncertain. It worried me that if Theseus had pressed his ship as we had ours he might already be in the High City. Surely he had no motive to hurry as we had hurried, but in my mind I kept seeing him getting out of a chariot at the foot of the Hill, Akama pale and silent beside him.

"Are horses taken right into the High City?" I asked Hyperes.

He shook his head. "Stables at the foot of the Hill, my lord. They could get horses up the road in an emergency, but it's too much of a nuisance for everyday. There's no room for them in the Acropolis and feed would have to be brought that much farther. They'd only take them up if the city were under a real siege. That hasn't happened in living memory."

As he said that I had a sudden image of Athens under siege. A mad image for the attackers seemed to be women in warrior garb. That image must be wrong, but it chilled me that my picture of Theseus getting out of his chariot at the foot of the Hill corresponded to facts that I had not been aware of. Still, perhaps that was still in the future and we might somehow have infiltrated the palace by that time.

It was growing dark as we came to the poor houses on the outskirts of Athens. As we threaded the crooked muddy streets I heard noises ahead of us: a spear hitting a shield with a dull ringing sound, the sould of heavy sandals on the road, the myriad little sounds that tell you that a body of armed men is near—a city patrol, probably, and coming right toward us!

Suddenly from a side lane the slender figure of a tall boy beckoned to us. For an instant, I almost thought that it was my brother Sarpedon, who was or should be safely home in Karia. But whoever the boy was and whatever his motive in beckoning to us, the side lane looked like a better bet than the main street we were on. At my low-voiced order our landing party followed the boy.

We pursued the fleeting figure down lanes that were hardly more than rutted paths between mean houses until we came to the end of a lane which led only to a house, small but a little bigger and better built than its neighbors. There was no sign of the boy, who had vanished around the bend just before we reached the house, but an old woman beckoned from the door and there was a lamp lit inside. I approached the door cautiously and was drawn inside by unexpectedly strong hands. The crude plank door creaked shut, leaving my men outside. The woman threw back the cloak that had shrouded her head and straightened up. In the light of the lamp I could see that the age lines on her face were cleverly applied face paint. Behind the paint was a face nothing could disguise from me, the face of Alceme, my mother!

We embraced fiercely for a moment and then her familiar voice sounded in my ear with the faintly insolent drawl that I knew often concealed her deeper emotions. "We'll catch up on news later, my son. For the moment we have to hurry. Theseus got back this morning. I saw who he had with him, so I know why you're here. Bring your men in here, quietly and quickly."

I opened the door and beckoned my men in. They crowded the little hut to overflowing. I said to them simply, "This is my mother, the Lady Alceme. Listen to her words and obey her in everything."

My mother faced us and spoke rapidly and incisively, in a low voice that carried to everyone in the hut but that would be indistinguishable outside it. "I played all over the Hill as a child. I am going to take you into the Acropolis by a way that very few people know about. But first we have to get past the lower guardpost. I am guesting with Menesthius and his wife in the Acropolis. The guards are going to think that I am being escorted from the wedding of some relation by some of the young men who are friends and relatives of the bride and groom. They are going to think this not because of anything we say but because you are going to act like wedding guests. There are garlands here and torches in the corner. There are also some jugs of wine. Wash your mouths out with it and sprinkle some on your clothing. You are going to be very drunk and very noisy and I am going to be scolding you loudly. If we do it right, the guards will laugh and wave us on. It wouldn't work for the gates of the Acropolis itself; they keep better watch there. But just because of that the road guards are careless. They know me, and if they're unsure of you they'll let the guards higher up worry about sending you back. Act your parts as if your lives depend on them. They do."

My mother can be very impressive when she wants to be, and we set out to follow her instructions with no delay. We left the little hut with one torch lit, but as we went we lit other torches from it. As we reached the road, Hyperes raised a bawdy wedding song and the others joined in raggedly, then began to laugh and give catcalls as they might have if they had over-celebrated at a real wedding. The men acting the parts of servants were quieter but acted tipsy too; the servants always get at the wine jugs after a party is in full swing. I walked beside my mother taking the part of someone's Kaphtui stewad ordered to make sure that the noble lady got safely home with or without the "help" of her drunken "escorts."

As we reached the guardpost my mother began abusing them fluently and amusingly for a lot of worthless drunken no-good sots. She managed to give the impression that she had drunk a few cups too many herself, and as we passed the grinning guards there were some rebald comments that they would not have dared make to her face.

One younger officer, more conscientous than the rest, said something to the captain, but I heard him say in a dismissing voice, "Let them go. The climb will sober them up. There'd be a brawl if we stopped them here—broken heads and hard feelings. At the Gates they'll let her slip in and leave them to caterwaul till they get tired of it."

We went around several bends, then my mother stopped us and with gestures of her hands like someone directing a chorus she told us to let our voices gradually fade away. At her quiet commands most of the torches were extinguished and we turned off the road and scrambled up the steep hillside. We stopped at a group of scrubby bushes, which she pushed aside to reveal a crack in the rock which seemed hardly big enough to admit a man. At her gesture we formed a circle around the crack, and she began unwinding rope from around her waist, under her cloak.

"We are going down into a hollow place in the hill," she said. "I'll go first and my son will come down after me carrying a torch. Come down after us in order of size. If any of you will not fit through the crack you still have an important job to do. Light the torches again and go down the hill, acting even drunker than before. Offer the guards wine, invite them back with you to the weding. The officer in charge will chase you away quickly just to be rid of you. Wait for us in the clump of trees below the cliff over there." She pointed. "If we can't get out any other way we may be coming over that cliff with ropes. You may have to fight off guards to let us get down safely."

She shrugged off her cloak and stood in a Dancer's kilt and boots. She threw the cloak down the crack and tied the rope to a tree with sailor's knots, knots which my father had taught to me and probably to her as well.

"Those who can't get down the crack must cut the rope as close to the knot as possible when the rest of us are down," she said. "We need the rope and there's no time to untie it in the dark." Then she vanished down the crack.

While I waited for the rope to stop moving, I tapped the shoulder of the biggest man in our group, a man who would never get through the crack. "You're in charge of those who stay behind, Koriano," I whispered. "Good luck."

He grasped my hand hard. "The gods go with you, my lord. After seeing your mother I know why you're the man you are. Leapers' luck to both of you."

The rope was steady then, and with a torch in my teeth I went down the rope hand over hand, using my feet around the rope to take a little weight off my arms. It was a long climb down, too long to climb up again even if the climb would bring us to a place not trapped between two guardposts. The torch threw fantastic shadows but I could see that we were in some kind of natural cave within the Hill. Then, when I came to the end of my climb down there was dressed stone under my feet and the remnants of a crude wooden stair leading away into the darkness.

My mother spoke in a whisper. "This is an old water supply in case of siege. There is a spring below us."

I could hear water dripping now, farther below than seemed possible. One by one the lighter and smaller men came down. After half a dozen had come down there was a pause. Finally one more man with scraped limbs and back came painfully down and the cut rope followed after another pause. Someone above with sense threw down several torches. The fall put them out but we lit them again from the one I had carried down.

With no more words, my mother beckoned us to follow her and, torches flaring in the gloom, we climbed the ruined stair. After a long climb she paused and gathered us around her. "We are below the temple of Athena," she said. "Here we stay until the dead of night. Then across the courtyard to the King" House and into Akama's room. Don't kill guards if you can help it, but there must be no outcry, no clash of arms. If you leave a man unconscious, leave him bound and gagged too. We can get to Akama, I'm sure of that. Getting off this Hill again will be the hard part. But these walls are meant to keep enemies out, not in. We may do it."

I spoke then. "If I once get to Akama, nothing will separate us again."

My mother looked into my face in the shifting torchlight. "I plan to see my grandchildren someday," she said with that faint drawl in her voice. "We'll get out again, one way or another." She wrapped her cloak around her and settled herself as comfortably as she could against the stones. "There's a little lamp on the shelf there, Akademus," she said in a low voice. "Light it and then put out the torches. Get what rest you can, all of you. Don't talk unless it's really necessary; sound might carry up into the temple and you can never tell who might be about."

I lit the lamp and then came up to the step where my mother was resting and settled down beside her. With a smile she settled herself against my shoulder and I fell into a fitful sleep, waking dozens of times to look around me in the flickering lamplight at the men wrapped in their cloaks, curled up wherever they could find a level place. Usually I would find my mother's eyes open when I woke, but I think we both managed to snatch a little sleep.

Chapter Fourteen
THE RESCUE

At last the lamp began to flicker and gutter out and my mother nodded to me. I went and touched the men to wake them. Most were awake already but a few had fallen soundly asleep and had to be shaken quietly with a hand at their mouths to keep them from crying out. We gathered in a tight circle and my mother spoke in a low flat voice that would not carry far.

"In a moment the lamp will go out and it will be time to start up again. It's not safe to use a light from here on up. Go up the stairs on hands and knees and touch the foot of the man ahead of you occasionally. By the time we get up, your eyes will be used to the darkness and you'll be able to see fairly well by the starlight in the courtyard. No talking from the time we leave here. When we get to the door of the temple watch me. I'll point in turn to each of the three guards we need to worry about. Akademus, choose a man for each guard…"

I held up two fingers. She nodded. "Two men for each guard. The first man should try to take care of the guard alone, the second is there in case the first has trouble. Don't kill if you can help it, but don't hesitate if you must. It may be our lives or theirs. When the guards are taken care of go to the corner of the King's House nearest the temple. The King's House is the only two-story building on the Hill, it's almost directly in front of the temple. Any questions?"

I looked from man to man in the flickering light, wishing I knew them better. The light gave one last flare and died to a feeble glow. We hastily formed a line and began creeping up the stairs. We went around several bends and then began a very steep climb. Presently my mother stopped and reached behind her to grasp my hand and draw me up beside her. With her mouth by my ear she breathed, "Wooden trapdoor. Lift. Slide toward me." She guided my hands to the right place on the smooth planks. We applied slow pressure until the trapdoor cleared the opening in which it was set, then slid it very gently and carefully to one side. My mother lifted herself up to the floor and moved noiselessly across it. I heard a tiny noise as she lifted a latch and then a door swung open letting in a little pale light. I beckoned to the men and we moved out of the little room with the trapdoor into the main part of the temple.

I felt a chill of awe as we passed the ancient wooden statue of Athena. The statue itself was only wood, but it had been the focus of many prayers and longing over the years. There must be a path somewhere in or near this building as there was near every major temple. If it weren't for the agreement that Theseus had extracted from me, help might have come down that path, but every path opens on both the Bright and the Dark worlds, and I couldn't help remembering the menace of the Dark Land and the deadly attractiveness of the Bright Land. Perhaps it was just as well that I could not could not call on the help of my Olympian friends. Any meddling with Immortals was dangerous and could have unforseen consequences. If I had not been drawn into Apollo's schemes, would Demeter still have devastated the fields of Kaphtu?

We were at the front entrance of the temple now, in the shadow of the massive wooden pillars that supported the pediment of the temple. The first guard was obvious enough, standing on the battlements silhouetted against the sky. The second was uncomfortably close to us, sheltering from the night wind against the far corner of the temple itself. The third was the hardest to see, standing near the steps on the King's House wrapped in his cloak.

The man on the battlements would be in one way the easiest, since he was looking outward and the courtyard below would be merely a mass of dark shadows to him. But he was farthest away and the approach to him would have to be slow and cautious. I touched the shoulders of my two best men, former Dancers from two and three years ago, and sent them for that guard. The man near the King's House would be the most difficult, since he was looking in our direction and his eyes were used to the dark at ground level. I sent Hyperes and his companion after this man, hoping that if the guard did see them, their Danaan nobleman's dress might make the guard hesitate just long enough. I gestured for the others to stay put and my mother and I slipped quietly toward the corner of the temple where the third guard sheltered.

When we were in position, I touched my mother's shoulder and she made a little low sound, halfway between a chuckle and a giggle. The guard turned toward her, no doubt expecting some amorous servant girl who had slipped out to tease the guards. As he turned, I hit him cleanly in the corner of the jaw and grabbed before he fell, easing him gently to the ground. Mother and I tied and gagged him quickly and efficiently, using sailor's knots and his own clothing. We then slipped back to where we could see the other two guards, leaving the guard we had attacked wrapped in his cloak and leaning against a corner of the wall. His sword, spear and shield I left out of his reach in the shadows of the porch.

As we watched intently, the guard on the battlements seemed to bend over suddenly and then could be seen no more. I silently congratulated myself on my choice of the two Dancers for that job. I had not heard a sound, and even if someone had seen the guard's movement, it could be explained by something like a broken sandal strap.

But now there was a scuffling noise from near the King's House—too loud and lasting too long. Waving my men after me, I ran across the courtyard. It was over by the time I got there, the guard dead with a knife in his back and Hyperes dying with a nasty woulnd in his stomach. Either he had bungled the attack or the guard had been unusually good. In any case it could not be helped now. We waited tensely for any reaction to the noise but as the silence continued we began to breathe again. My mother took something small from her sash—I could not see what in the dim light—and lobbed it expertly up into the second-story window just above us. It made a tiny rattle on the floor of the room above and again we all held our breath waiting for any reaction.

After a moment a rope came down from the window above, lowered quickly but not thrown. It made no noise at all. My mother gestured me up and I climbed the wall with the aid of the rope, my now bare feet making no sound. In a moment I was in the room above and Akama was in my arms, clinging to me desperately. My mother had come up the rope after me and was busy with the rope, making a knot that would stand a steady strain but could be freed with the right kind of twist and jerk.

We all froze as we heard a noise at the door, the pin being taken out of the latch, then the latch being lifted. In the light of a small lamp which he carried in one hand I saw the face I had last seen across a narrow lane of water, holding a sword to his daughter's breast: Theseus, King of Athens! He had a sword in one hand and a reckless grin on his face.

"Well played, boy, and almost won. I'm almost tempted to relent, but I want no more Cretan blood in my family. Now we'll just..." He broke off as my mother rose from where she had been crouching. Somewhere along the way she had removed the old woman's disguise from her face and standing there in her Dancer's kilt she riveted his attention for one vital moment. "The blonde bull Leaper," he began. "How did..."

But Akama, with one fluid movement seized and hurled a heavy water jug at his head and I was on top of him in a second with Akama and my mother after me. Half-dazed by the water jug, his breath knocked out of him by my jump and up against the trained muscles of three Leapers, the mighty Theseus was

trussed and gagged before he knew what had
happened. Before we left him in the corner behind
Akama's bed, covered over with the bedclothes, I
pulled off his tunic, a very distinctive one. His eyes
were shut—he was either unconscious or shaming—
but he wouldn't get out of our knots in a hurry. I bent
over him for a moment. "Farewell Theseus," I
murmured. "You should have fought me when I
offered you the chance." Then we were out of the
window, Akama first, then my mother, then myself.

A twist and jerk and the rope was in our hands and,
leaving the body of Hyperes with that of the guard, our
whole group was moving toward the spot on the
battlements where the first guard had stood. If Theseus
had been foolish enough to check whatever noises he
had heard without sending for help, we might still
make it over the wall. We had tied the two ropes
together and secured them to the battlements when
men with torches poured from the King's House.
Another moment and we might have made it, but we
were spotted and a voice rang out, "Stand where you
are. We have archers. Try to move and you'll be
spitted."

I whispered to Akama, "Distract them for a
moment," grabbed the man in our company who
looked most like Theseus and bundled him into the
tunic I had pulled from the captive king. I swathed his
head in a cloak and whispered instructions: he was to
pretend that his arms were bound and that he was half-
stunned.

While I was doing this behind the screen formed by
the bodies of my men, Akama stepped forward into the

light of the torches and called out, "Uncle Menesthius, that's you, isn't it?"

A semicircle of armed men was now around us and from their ranks a man stepped. His tunic was simple and under his grizzled hair his face was thoughtful and sensible, but he had an air of complete authority. Akama went on. "Uncle Menesthius, you know that in tearing me away from my husband, my father broke the laws of Kaphtu: the Ariadne has the right to choose her husband. Rather than go back now, I'd leap over this wall with my husband. Let us go and end the bloodshed and folly."

Menesthius's voice was full of pain as he said, "I'm sorry, Akama, but I'm your father's man. I can't break my oaths. If you surrender now I'll speak for you to Theseus…"

I stepped out into the light then, dragging the man I had crudely disguised as Theseus and hoping no forgotten detail would give me away. "He's not in much condition to listen, Menesthius," I said. "Do you still want to spit us on your arrows? Put down your weapons or I'll throw him over the battlements. I'd rather trust your justice than his."

My mother came forward to stand beside "Menesthius, you know me;" she said. "Two men have died tonight because of Theseus's madness. Do you think I'd hesitate to kill him rather than let him kill my son? If you let us go freely you'll find Theseus safe and sound in the morning, you have my word on it. Refuse and we'll try to get over the wall. Do you think he'll survive?" She gestured toward the false Theseus who gave a lunge toward her and was grabbed by two of my men. I blessed the man—a good piece of acting.

Menesthius hesitated, then nodded slowly. "You have my safe conduct off the Hill. What orders Theseus will give when he's free again I can guess, although you won't get far with an unwilling captive. You may be only postponing your fate. But it would serve no purpose to have a general carnage here."

My mother nodded. "He goes over the wall to our friends below. They have their orders, and if we don't come for him they'll carry them out. I trust your word, Menesthius, but I don't trust him." She tied a loop of the rope around the body of the false Theseus and we lowered him hand-over-hand down the wall. As soon as he was out of sight, the man could use his hands to fend himself off, so it was not as bad a journey for him as it would have been for a man whose arms were really bound.

With a sense of unreality I found myself walking beside the grizzle-headed Menesthius through the main gate and down the Hill by the path.

Akama was the first to speak. "Give our man who died in the attack a decent burial, uncle, she said. "Who was he, Ducalion?

I took her hand in mine. "Hyperes, one of the plotters you banished to their estates. He's paid his debts."

She nodded somberly. "Yes," she said in a small voice. "I suppose he volunteered. I'm sorry about the guard."

Menesthius's voice was gentle as he said, "It's a soldier's job to give his life in defense of his post.

157

These troubles started long ago, perhaps with M'nos, perhaps even before then. Don't blame yourself."

My mother spoke then. "I've given you and T'ne poor return for my guesting, Menesthius, but you can understand that I had no choice."

Menesthiusís voice was dry as he said, I'm sure T'ne will understand, Alceme."

I remembered that T'ne was a former Leaper and an old friend of my mother's. As the wife of Menesthius, Theseus's chief lieutenant, she was for all intents and purposes the first lady of Athens and would have access anywhere. I wondered if T'ne had been the means by which that rope had gotten into Akama's room, a suspicion that was strengthened when Menesthius continued, "You women have a different attitude to those things than men. Perhaps a more sensible one."

We were at the bottom of the Hill now and Menesthius turned and faced me. "Theseus boasted to me of the promise he wrung out of you. I'd say you've kept your part of the bargain; you got Akama off the Hill without help from the Olympians. But don't expect Theseus to give you his blessing, as he promised. He might if he were in his right mind, but he isn't. Akama will tell you why. He hesitated and bit his lip, then seemed to come to some decision. "The sooner you're out of his way the better," he said. He swung around and, with a gesture for us to follow him, led the way to a low building from which came an unmistakably horsey smell.

At his orders a chariot was wheeled out and two horses put to it. "I can't ask for more without arousing suspicion," he said in a low voice. "This chariot's meant to carry two armed men; it should carry the three of you. Take it and ride like Hades. Don't tell me where. I don't want to know. Good luck! He embraced Akama, briefly took my hand and my mother's and strode away.

Under the curious eyes of the stableboys and guards we mounted the chariot. We were all swathed in cloaks, but Akama and my mother were obviously women, and the guards looked to Menesthius curiously. But his authority was unquestioned and we trotted away from the Hill, our men running behind us, without anyone trying to stop us. As soon as we were out of sight of the guards, I sent one of the men to collect the rest of our party from the little patch of woods at the foot of the Hill.

My mother and Akama had been conferring and Akama spoke now: "Tell them to meet us at the foot of Lycabettos." She pointed to the curiously shaped little hill that faced the Hill of Athens across the valley. "We'll go first and the men can follow as swiftly as they can."

The men saluted and we set off at a canter, soon leaving the men behind. About halfway across the valley my mother glanced up at the hill and said laconically, "Whip up the horses, Akademus. From the lights and shouts up there I think they've found Theseus."

Chapter Fifteen
THE GROVE

I forced the pace a little, but in the dark and on unfamiliar roads I could not go much faster. Akama was clinging to me with both her arms around me. Occasionally she was racked by a shudder. But her eyes were open and she gave me a good warning of every turn to take.

My mother stood braced to the movement of the chariot, with one hand lightly on the rail. Her mouth was open slightly in a little smile that showed her teeth. She looked as if she were enjoying herself. I knew I was seeing the girl who had been a Leaper of bulls, the wife and mother of the intervening years temporarily submerged.

As we neared the foot of Lycabettos we came to a little grove of trees. "Stop here," said Akama and very slowly and reluctantly she removed her arms from around me. "Wait here, my love," she said a little unsteadily. "Don't go away." She looked at my mother. "Will you come with me?" she asked.

My mother shook her head. "Better go alone," she said.

Akama jumped from the chariot, touched my hand lightly with a little smile and ran into the grove. I went to the horses' heads and looked at my mother, still in the chariot. "We ought to walk the horses if she'll be long," I said.

My mother shook her head. "She won't be. And when she returns I must take the chariot and go on." She raised a hand to still my protest. "We don't have much time, Akademus. Tell me everything that happened since you left Karia, the essential things, I mean. I know some of it but leave nothing out. Some detail might be vital.

I stroked the horses to calm them as I marshaled the facts in my mind and then reported, briefly and concisely as my father had taught me. My mother asked a few questions all about my trip to the Dark Land. She brooded for a moment and then spoke.

"I'm not taking the chariot on just to draw pursuit away from you, though it will have that effect," she said. "I have to get back to the palace of King Ceseus in Eleusis." At my inquiring look she gave me an impish grin. "I'm a serving woman there, though admittedly rather an upper servant. We just took on a new nursemaid for the king's baby son. A woman who says she's from Kaphtu, says that she was stolen by pirates and escaped when they landed for water on the coast near Eleusis. I think you might recognize the woman, Akademus. You last met her in a field near N'sos."

"Demeter?" I gasped. "What on earth is she doing in Eleusis?" Eleusis is a tiny Attilkan kingdom near Athens. The only remarkable thing about it that I knew of was that it had always managed to keep free of the rule of Athens, its larger and more powerful neighbor.

My mother's face was somber. "Meditating mischief, very likely," she said. "There's a path near the palace in Eleusis, a very ancient and important path, maybe even the path that Cronos first walked to the Bright Land. Her presence at Eleusis has something to do with that, we think." At my lifted eyebrows she explained, "Britomortis and I. My job is to keep an eye on Demeter, to find out if I can what she's up to and to distract her if I can. I've already had some success. I made her laugh." At my incredulous stare she nodded somberly. "Making her laugh is no laughing matter, Akademus. She is a daughter of Cronos, a Great Olympian, one of the most dangerous and powerful beings in the Three Worlds. And the loss of her daughter has sent her very close to madness. Anything that will make her more normal, a baby, a joke, may stave off disaster for a little longer. My job is to stay close to her and watch, call Brit and the others if things go wrong. She won't suspect a mortal, you see. She's one of the Olympians who despise mortals rather. But I find myself liking her, oddly enough. If someone stole M'pha from me as Persephone was stolen from her I might strike out as she is doing."

I shook my head. "Not if M'pha loved her abductor as Persephone loves Adis," I said.

My mother smiled a slightly crooked smile. "Perhaps not. But then I've never been as wrapped up in my children as Demeter was in Persephone. That does mean I'm not fond of you though, my son. Take care of yourself and Akama. I still want to see those grandchildren. Speaking of Akama, here she comes and I think she's been successful."

Akama came running out of the grove, bright faced, and said happily, "The Wild Ones will give us sanctuary. The men can stay in the grove and the three of us can go into the shrine."

My mother shook her head. "The two of you. I have to go. Your husband will explain." She stepped from the chariot and embraced Akama warmly. "I approve of you, daughter. Don't let anything happen to you or this son of mine. As I just told him, I want to see some grandchildren." Then she leaped into the chariot, whipped up the horses and was gone.

"She and Britomartis are up to something," I told Akama. "I'll explain later. I suppose we'd better wait here for the men to catch up with us."

She nodded and came into my arms and we leaned against a tree holding each other and kissing for awhile like country lovers. Then she began talking. I could tell from her tone that something weighed on her mind that she had to talk out. I held her tightly and listened.

"Do you know why my father never did anything about our betrothal until a little while ago, Ducalion? It was because of my mother and my half-brother, Hyppolytus, the Amazon princess's son. Mother was always jealous of him. He was half-grown when she married father and I suppose she saw him as a threat to her own position in some way. Mother worried about things like that a great deal. I don't know why, perhaps it was having been born the second daughter, not the heiress, that made her so determined to hold onto her power once she got it. That's why I once thought that she and father might have—done something—to Ariadne, do you remember?"

I murmured assent and held her closer and she went on, speaking in the same strained voice. "Hyppolytus was a strange boy, very obedient and conventional in some things but very strange in other ways. Father had him hidden away with friends as a boy and when he brought him to Athens after he

163

became king the two never became really close. I think Hyppolytus really preferred the company of Artimodorus, the man who was Tauromath the year after Britomartis. They'd go off into the wilderness together for long periods and Hyppolytus learned a lot about animals from Artimodorus, though I don't think he had Tauromathic powers himself. Hyppolytus was a big handsome boy, good at all kinds of games and sports, but he always seemed uneasy with people. Father was proud of him but a little puzzled by him."

"Aunt Brit said that Artimodorus's mother was a priestess of Artemis. The Amazons are devotees of Artemis, so I suppose that made some sort of link between them," I suggested.

Akama nodded abstractedly and went on. "Anyway, Hyppolytus was even shyer with women than with men and father couldn't understand that very well." She gave a little crooked smile.

I wondered compassionately what her childhood had been with her jealous, insecure mother and her father's proclivity for all kinds of adventures, including amorous ones. Her voice showed added strain now and I knew she was coming to the hardest part of her narrative.

"I don't know if my mother was genuinely attracted to him or was simply trying to lure him into doing something that would get him in trouble with father, but apparently for the most part of this year she was acting in a very un-stepmotherly way toward Hyppolytus—teasing him, tempting him, almost forcing him to think of her as a woman. Aunt T'ne told me that and I trust her. But I don't know what was

164

behind it. Perhaps no more than boredom. My mother could get up to all kinds of deviltry when she was bored."

She paused and then forced herself to go on "I don't know what happened, perhaps no one will ever know, but, apparently, not long before we banished Euphoros my mother accused Hyppolytus to my father. Apparently she accused him of trying to rape her. I don't know if she claimed he'd succeeded or not. Anyway, father flew into one of his rages. Hyppolytus decided to leave Athens—not from cowardice, I think, but to avoid a fight with his own father. But it looked to father like an admission of guilt. He pursued Hyppolytus down to the port at Phaleron, and when the ship looked like it would get clear of his pursuit, father called on his own true father, Posudi. They say that the ship Hyppolytus was in was smashed into splinters by a great creature like a bull that appeared from the depths of the sea. The rest of the crew were picked up out of the sea, but Hyppolytus was never found." She paused and then said with a little touch of bitter humor. "No wonder that when Euphoros came back to Athens not long after he didn't find father very interested in his stories about us."

She went on in a somber tone. "As the summer went on, my father gradually began to wonder whether he'd been unfair to Hyppolytus, then he put the blame on my mother. He began to turn against Kaphtu itself: told the Argives that his protection was withdrawn from it, swore that his daughter would never marry anyone of Kaphtui blood. It was as if he were trying to undo what he had done in marrying my mother, rejecting the kngdom he had won by marrying her as well as rejecting my mother herself. That was one reason why he kidnapped me. The other was that he had become obsessed with proving my mother's guilt. He wanted…he wanted to use my Power of Truth to discover what had really happened with Hyppolytus."

I could feel her muscles tense and I knew the worst, whatever that was, was still to be told. It came in a rush: "No one will ever know now. When my mother heard that my father's ship had docked in Phaleron she hanged herself. We found her dead this morning when we reached the High City."

She clung to me then, a storm of weeping interrupted with great gasps for breath. I let her cry herself out, but when she started to say something incoherent about not wanting to entangle me with such a family, I interrupted her gently but firmly. "Akama, my love, don't talk nonsense. You know what Ariadne's mother was; you know what the Dark M'nos was. You know what Ariadne is like; you know that Dion chose her for his bride. Your parents hurt each other and I can see that they've both hurt you, deeply, but that has nothing to do with you, or with you and me. If you don't trust my judgment, trust Ariadne's and my mother's. They both approve of you. But if they didn't it wouldn't matter. Nothing is going to separate us again and you know it as well as I do."

It was not up to Lykos's standards of logic, perhaps, but it satisfied Akama, and by the time our men arrived at the grove she was more like her old self, her grief and shock already half eased by the telling of her story and by our reunion.

We gathered the men around us and told them that the nymphs of this place gave them permission to shelter in the Holy Grove; where of course they would be safe. No one would suspect that any male would dare to enter it, and even if it were known that they were there, no one but a madman would attempt to violate their sanctuary. The men filed into the grove casting apprehensive looks about them, but the last man seemed to be stopped by some mysterious force when he tried to enter the grove. I stepped closer to see him better. It was the companion of Hyperes, the other of the two conspirators who had begged to come with me.

"I expected this, my lord," the man said. "I was the man who killed the guard after he got Hyperes. The Holy Place will not admit a man with blood fresh on his hands, I know Attika, lord, I can get back to the ship across country, if you wish me to."

I nodded slowly. "All right. Tell them to leave Piraeus and dock in Phaleron as if they had just come from the sea. We'll try to join the ship tomorrow night. No one will expect the ship that brought us to sail boldly into Phaleron, and I think we have a chance to get aboard in the dark if we seem to have vanished tonight and tomorrow. If we don't make it tomorrow, let them make a show of trading and wait two more nights. If we aren't back by then, they are free to return to Kaphtu." He saluted and melted into the darkness.

Akama and I walked through the grove to the little bower that was the Shrine of the Nymphs. Someone had prepared a couch for us there and though the air seemed full of the strangeness of the Wild Ones, that seemed to dispel shyness rather than causing it. It was not quite the joyful union we had hoped for in our own little valey, but we had a great need of each other and a great longing to be united at last. We have had many more joyous unions since, but perhaps none deeper or more tender. There in the Sacred Grove within sight of her fatherís stronghold, Akama became my wife in truth.

That night and the next day remain in my memory as a time spent almost as much outside the everyday world as my time in the Dark Land and my brief glimpse of the Bright Land. Some influence of the Wild Ones, some air from Olympus, removed our griefs and problems and we wandered in that grove as if it were a world apart, as perhaps it was, for it seemed larger than it could in fact have been and no sight or sound of the world outside reached us there. We wandered hand in hand between trees and beside streams, and before night fell again I heard Akama's laugh again, and saw the light back in her eyes.

Our men, too, seemed rested and at peace when we left the grove under the faint light of a new moon, with a strange light in their eyes. None told me what he had experienced, or dreamed, in that grove, but they left with almost as much reluctance as Akama and I. We walked in silence down deserted roads and I think the Fear of the Wild Ones went with us, for every living thing seemed to avoid us until we found ourselves in the faint light of dawn on the dock at Phaleron, with our ship before us.

They were on the alert and as soon as we were all aboard rowers were at their benches, the cable was slipped and we were rowing out to sea. But the protection of the Wild Ones seemed to stop at the water's edge: as soon as we were under way there were shouts and challenges from other ships. The strange isolation that had protected us from the moment we had left the grove was broken.

We ignored the challenges and kept steadily out to sea, breaking out the sail as soon as the wind served. We were hoping that the mere fact of a ship leaving unexpectedly would not in itself draw pursuit, that orders would have to be issued by someone, perhaps even by someone in Athens before ships would be sent after us.

At first we seemed to be getting away clean, and as minute followed minute with no sign of pursuit our hearts lifted. We would soon be far enough ahead of any possible pursuers so that with good seamanship we could keep ahead of them all the way to Kaphtu. This late in the sailing season the weather would be capricious, but we counted on Kaphtui sailing skills to turn this to our advantage.

At first, we were glad to see the storm clouds. No successful pursuit could be mounted in rain and high winds. But presently the wind grew stronger and the seas higher. The captain, Akama and I began to look at each other with mounting worry. The storm had arisen too quickly and was not acting like a normal storm at sea. The winds and waves seemed to batter at us from all sides and the ship became harder and harder to control.

Akama said in a low voice, "If my father has called on Posudi again..." As she uttered the god's name a tremendous gust of wind ripped the sail to shreds and winds began tearing at the ship, forcing it off its course. The useless oars were shipped, and we clung to the ship for dear life, riding out the storm, at the mercy of wind and wave, in danger of swamping at any moment and being forced to some unknown destination.

Chapter Sixteen
THE SHIPWRECK

I have never been able to calculate how many days we ran before that storm, played with by wind and wave. Luckily there were four of us aboard who had some experience as steersmen, and we took short shifts, keeping the ship head to the wind to avoid being broached and swamped. Each steersman had a helper to throw his weight on the steering oar at the steersman's command. When my turns came Akama took her place beside me. The rest of the men aboard bailed whenever they were not trying to rest. We lived on hard bread and olives, washed down with straight wine for warmth. There was no question, of course, of lighting cooking fires.

Akama and I huddled together for warmth when we were not at the oar together. Like everyone aboard ship, we were soaked to the skin, but it was not too cold except in the hours just before dawn. We had little to do except talk. The fury of the storm made it useless to take any of the measures that I would normally have ordered on a storm-beset ship. We tried setting sea anchors a few times, but each time the sea twitched away our makeshift constructions contemptuously. Anything that carried away in the wind had to be left unrepaired and there was no lull in which we could have passed cables around the ship to keep her from breaking up. Her timbers held, but increasingly gaped wider and lost their caulking. Despite our best efforts, our bailing began to fall behind the water that entered the ship, and we sank lower and lower into the water.

Akama and I agreed that her father had called on Posudi again. This storm was too fierce and prolonged to be natural. The only question was whether the Sea Lord would kill us or only punish us. When we finally heard the sound of breakers on a shore we were still uncertain. Being dashed on a shore would almost surely be the end of the ship and of us but we could have been swamped and sunk at sea any time during the past days if Posudi wanted our lives. Still, as the breakers grew louder Akama and I clung together, knowing that this might be our last moment.

As the shore loomed before us, a slender figure stood beside us on the afterdeck. It was the youth with a look of my brother who had led our raiding party to where my mother had waited, and a suspicion I had had then sudddenly became certainty. I raised my voice above the storm. "Aunt Brit, is that you?"

She nodded incisively, the movement somehow completely hers despite her disguise. "Be prepared to jump when the ship breaks up," she said. "Posudi will spare your lives but not the ship."

There was no time to reply. The ship struck then with a terrible crunching sound and a groan of tortured timbers. Akama and I used the momentum to jump, hand in hand, clear of the ship. Once in the water I felt myself grasped by a hand stronger than that of any mortal. We were half carried, half dragged through a welter and foam and deposited on the beach above the waterline just in time to turn and see a great wave hit our stranded ship like a battering ram. The ship literally exploded, timbers flying high in the air.

Akama and I rushed back down to the waterline to drag out crew members who had been washed ashore like flotsam. Farther down the beach Aunt Brit in her boy's disguise was doing the same. The winds began to die down and the waves to calm, as if they had been appeased by the destruction of our ship. As we assembled our half-drowned crew on the beach, I saw with a heavy heart that not a single one of the men who had been on the raiding party with me had survived the waves. I told Akama this and found Aunt Brit at my elbow, listening. She nodded, her disguised face grim and compassionate.

"They spent their last nights ashore in the arms of the nymphs at the shrine where you sheltered," she said softly. "I think they would not have lived long in any case." I remembered that the men had been silent, almost entranced, ever since we had left the shrine.

Now that we were all out of the water I looked around for some sort of shelter for us. The wind was dying with the storm, but Akama was beginning to shiver partly from cold and partly from the shock of our shipwreck. As I looked up to the hills above the beach, I saw a line of men coming down a path. I stared, hardly beliving my eyes, for they were leading a great black bull and were dressed in Danaan festival finery. Their leader was a tall, slightly grizzled man with an air of quiet authority. As the group reached us he gave us a salute as ceremonious as if we had been an embassy, rather than a group of bedraggled shipwrecked sailors.

"Welcome to Pylos," he said formally. "We were coming to the shore to make sacrifice to King Posudi, since this storm seemed to be no ordinary one, and perhaps was a sign from the god." I saw that the bull's horns were gilded for sacrifice, and one of the attendants was carrying a sacrificial axe. "We can now offer the bull to the Sea Lord in thanksgiving for your escape," he continued. Hardly were the words out of his mouth when the bull began to plunge and rear, lunging at us as if to attack. His handlers were caught by surpnse and for a moment it looked as if the bull would get away, but Akama and Aunt Brit each stepped forward and each took one horn of the bull. He immediately returned to his former placidity and the men around him stepped back and regarded us with awe.

Their leader looked at us with mingled respect and suspicion. "Who are you, strangers, that escape the threat of the sea only to be threatened by the sacred bull? Are you gods yourselves or enemies of gods that you face these perils and yet escape them?"

Britomartis stepped forward and, although she still wore her disguise as a young man scarcely out of boyhood, there was something about her as she stood there that caused every eye to be fixed on her with apprehension and respect.

"It is well to respect the gods, Nestor, king of sandy Pylos," she said. "But as you well know a mortal may incur the wrath of the Olympians through no fault of his own. At the prayer of Theseus, his son, King Posudi drove these travelers from their course and wrecked their ship. But he has spared their lives at the request of his niece, Pallas Athene, Lady of Triton. Now that they have reached land they are under her protection. Treat them with respect. This lady at my side is Akama, the Ariadne of Crete, and yonder stands her husband, Ducalion, First Councillor of Karia. Theseus has abandoned his rule of Crete, and if King Posudi's wrath can be appeased so that they can reach their home, they will be the rulers of the fair land of Crete. Treat them as you wish the Lady Triton to treat you."

With these words, the form that Britomartis wore seemed to change into that of a great sea bird which circled thrice around our heads and flew off into the sky.

I looked into the eyes of Nestor, King of Pylos, and said, "No king who rules ships on the sea wants to offend King Posudi, my lord. If you would rather not receive us…"

He grinned suddenly and gave me a ceremonial embrace of welcome. "Your friends seem as formidable as your enemies, King Ducalion," he said. "I will take my chances on the Sea Lord's anger, which can die as suddenly as it flares up. If he does not wish to accept this fine bull, I will offer it up to the Lady of Triton on your behalf. You are my guests and a guest is sacred. A man can only do what he thinks is right and hope that the gods will be appeased by sacrifice."

At his gesture, servants began to lay fires while the handlers led the bull forward. King Nestor himself took the axe and dropped the bull with one mighty stroke. Akama winced and so did I. A Dancer cannot regard a bull as merely meat, but I knew that we would have to accept and eat with good grace the choice portions that would be offered to us as guests of honor.

At least they dragged the bull off down the beach for butchering.

We stood near the fire, grateful for its warmth, while the thigh bones of the bull, wrapped in fat, were burned in sacrifice. We were offered wine in a great doublehanded golden cup. I drank and returned the cup to Nestor, who offered it with a bow to Akama. When she returned it, it was taken by a handsome boy, about the age that Aunt Brit had appeared to be, with a marked resemblance to Nestor. My guess was confirmed when Nestor said with ill-concealed pride, "This young rascal is Antilochus, my son. Greet our guests, boy."

Antilochus gave us a merry grin and saluted us in Kaphtui fashion. "I hope you will welcome me in your own halls some day, my lord and lady," he said. "If I can ever convince my father that I am grown up I hope to travel and see some of the world."

"You will be very welcome, Prince Antilochus," I said and Akama added with a warm smile, "Any traveler from Pylos of the White Sands will be thrice welcome in our House of N'sos, Antilochus. We hope to greet you there soon." I felt a little chill of apprehension at those words. If Posudi continued to bar the seas to us it might be a long time before we ourselves reached our island kingdom.

Now sheepskins were spread on the sand for us to sit on and we were given such warm clothing as could be found for us among the men from Pylos. Under the cover of a heavy cloak, Akama slipped out of the drenched Danaan dress she had been wearing ever since she had left her father's palace. One of the servants came up with a fine piece of cloth that had perhaps been intended to be spread out under plates of food. She wrapped it around her and I helped fasten it with the shoulder pins from her old dress. I myself was given a spare tunic of the king's, brought along in case the blood from the sacrifice splattered the one he was wearing.

Most of the men in King Nestor's party treated us with the greatest respect, but I noticed that a little group of men who clustered around their own fire and had offered their own sacrilices kept darting hostile glances at us. When Nestor looked at them his face was troubled. As the feast ended men began getting up to stretch their legs and relieve themselves behind some nearby bushes. Young Antilochus helped Akama to her feet with a courteous bow and the three of us strolled a little way down the beach, looking out at the now peaceful waters which had so nearly killed us.

As soon as we were out of earshot of the others, Antilochus spoke in a low urgent voice. "My lord and lady, my father would not trouble you with this news, but I think you should know. Those men who kept looking at you so discourteously are envoys from the Argive King at Mykenae. They came to ask my father to take part in a great raid on Crete. If he had agreed they were to sail tomorrow!"

Richard Purtill

Chapter Seventeen
THE GUARDIAN

That news would have disturbed our sleep if anything could, but by the time Nestor had led us up the cliff path, where we were met by chariots which carried us to his palace, we were asleep on our feet. We could hardly keep awake for courteous protests when the king led us to his own finely carved wooden bedstead and told us we would not be disturbed until we called. We slipped out of our clothes and curled up in each other's arms under the bedclothes, too exhausted to do more than exchange a sleepy kiss.

We made up for that in the morning, and the sun was high in the sky when we summoned the servants, Akama was led away by giggling maidservants and I was taken to the bath where my back was scrubbed by the king's daughters: Danaan hospitality. They modestly turned their eyes away when I emerged from the tub, but I caught the younger sneaking a peek and whispering to her more straitlaced sister who smiled and blushed. I was clothed in a tunic of soft lambswool, dyed a deep blue and embroidered in gold, and given sandals with gilded edges. The two daughters of Nestor returned with a finely embroidered sash and a belt-knife worth a year's trading. It had a lovely leaping dolphin inlaid in the blade with gold and enamel.

I thanked them ceremoniously but gave the younger one a grin to let her know I had seen her actions earlier: she had the grace to blush. The two of them took my hands and led me to the great hall of the palace. Nestor was seated on a high-backed chair not unlike the Sea King's throne in Kaphtu. Both thrones were modeled after the high-backed chair of a sea captain, somewhat more richly carved and decorated. The people here were very likely a mixture of the Old People, related to the Children of Kariatu on Kaphtu, Pelesgian sea raiders and the Danaans who in turn had conquered them and settled among them. It was the usual mixture on the islands near the sea; only in the Argolid did the fiercer race of the north predominate.

Two ladies in long robes not unlike Kaphtui garb, except that the jackets closed over their breasts, were seated near the circular hearth. It took me a second to realize that one was Akama. I saluted her formally and just as formally she introduced me to Anaxibia, the queen. In many of the older kingdoms, the palace, and sometimes the fields, too, are reckoned as belonging to the queen. I took a chance on offending Nestor and thanked Anaxibia for welcoming us to her house before thanking Nestor himself for his kindness in rescuing us from the shore. She smiled graciously and Nestor showed no signs of taking offense, so we had passed one test successfully. Antilochus, sitting on a low-backed chair beside his father, gave me a friendly smile. The Argive envoys were nowhere in sight, though many of the ladies and gentlemen of the court were in the room, strolling up and down or talking quietly on the benches near the walls.

Visitors are expected to pay for hospitality with the latest news, and when Nestor had a chair brought for me and courteously questioned Akama and me about our travels, the courtiers gathered around to listen. It

179

was no use concealing our troubles with Theseus, so I told them of Akama's kidnapping and my expedition to rescue her. I did not want to say too much of my mother's part or reveal that we had hidden in the shrine of the nymphs, so my own part in things sounded more impressive than in fact it had been. Nestor regarded me with increased respect and I supressed any impulse to be modest. I needed this man's friendship.

When I had finished my story, Nestor looked for a moment at Anaxibia, and the two seemed to commune with their eyes. My own eyes sought Akama's and found reassurance there. When Nestor turned back to me I met his gaze steadily.

"Lord M'nos," he began, and my heart leapt, for by giving me the title he showed that he meant to treat me as a fellow monarch, "you and your lady are our guests for as long as you wish to stay. Whoever offends you in any way offends me. I would offer you ships to take you home but I fear the seas are no place for you now. There are raiders at sea who would like well to have you as hostages, and Posudi's anger is not likely to be appeased by a storm and a shipwreck. I am a descendant of Posudi myself and I do not think that he will vent his anger on my ships in general, but until the Sea Lord's wrath has cooled. I would not like to be aboard any ship that carried you."

Nestor's words were kind and they meant that Akama and I were personally safe, but if we could not cross the seas to reach our island kingdom, the palace of Nestor was like a gilded prison for us. Neither Akama nor I was likely to rest very comfortably in Pylos while Argive raiders and Demeter's blight threatened our people. They had given us their loyalty for no better reason than ancestry and our skill at bull-leaping and we owed them whatever service we could give them.

As soon as Akama and I could be alone together I wanted to discuss plans, but as guests we were bound to let ourselves be entertained by our hosts. I toured the royal stables and watched the soldiers of Pylos at practice with Antilochus and had some good conversations with Nestor, who was a trader and farmer as well as a ruler, like most of these small kings. I learned with a chill of foreboding that a blight was appearing in the fields of Pylos and that the priestesses if Rhea and Demeter had issued dark warnings of worse to come.

Akama confirmed this when we finally had a chance to talk, in bed that night. We were still in the bedchamber of Nestor and Anaxibia, but a small annex to the palace was already being redecorated for us. It was kind, but it had a dismaying air of permanence. Akama told me that Anaxibia was a priestess of Ria. Akama herself, as the Ariadne of Kaphtu, was a major priestess of the Mother and she had been treated with considerable respect by Anaxibia. The omens from Ria and her daughter, Demeter, were even darker than Nestor knew.

Akama told me with a grin, "Anaxibia loves Nestor, but she doesn't trust him as I trust you."

We had a long frustrating discussion before we sought comfort in each other's arms. We could probably make our way by land to Karia, but that did not solve the problem of getting back to our kingdom, and the journey would have many perils. If Posudi had given his son Theseus some promise concerning us, the seas might be closed to us for a long time, even aside from the danger of running into the Argive invasion fleet. I trusted Apollo's promise to defend the coast of Karia, but the thought of those sea wolves on the prowl around my country gave me little joy. The trading season was largely over but there were belated ships which might be snapped up and Kaphtui trading sites on other islands which would be vulnerable.

Talk as we would, there was only one thing to do. Neither of us liked disturbing the Olympians; our dealings with them had made us realize how easy it was to court disaster by meddling with them. Would Demeter have cursed the fields of Kaphtu if I had not run Apollo's errand for him? Now there was no way to avoid it. To evade Posudi's apparent ban on our return home we would have to call on our friends in Olympus.

Apollo owed me a debt, but to Akama's obvious relief I immediately rejected any idea of calling on him. Ariadne and Aunt Brit owed me nothing, but I would rather be in their debt than claim my due from Apollo and perhaps be involved in his schemes again. I only hoped that one of my friends would be free to help. I knew that the Olympians were not all powerful, and Ariadne and Aunt Brit were somehow involved in the attempt to deal with Demeter that my mother had told me a little of.

Akama found out from Anaxibia the location of the nearest shrine that was likely to contain a Path; not that she asked in those terms, of course. Our request to visit the shrine and spend some time alone there caused no great surprise. Rulers are expected to speak to the gods on behalf of their people. When we were alone we linked hands and concentrated on the thought of our Olympian friends. I, at least, was thinking mainly of Aunt Brit, whom I had seen only in that one brief glimpse on the scene of the shipwreck since my adventures began. But when, after a nerve-wrecking wait, a familiar golden sparkle appeared in the depths of the cave shrine where we stood, it was Ariadne who appeared.

She looked as nearly harried and worried as I had ever seen her, although her smile was warm. "We haven't forgotten you two," she said, "but this businesss wih Demeter seems to go from one crisis to another. We don't have time to get around Posudi on your behalf. Normally Brit can twist him around her finger; now he's saying he gave his word to Theseus to sink any ship that he saw taking you to Kaphtu. So I thought of a plan that might work and Brit asked her aunt to reweave the Thread—only 'Thena could have done it. Oh, you don't know what I'm talking about, of course. Akama, this is an old treasure of our House that I'm restoring to you. K'demus, this is the Veil of Adis that Brit and I have told you stories about."

She gently laid in Akama's outstretched hands something which I could not see; I could only tell from the way Akama's hands dropped and her fingers gripped that there was anything passed from one to the other. I laid my hands on the invisible bundle and felt a curious thrill and a slight sensation of cold.

"The Veil of Adis," Akama murmured softly, and I knew that she too had heard of the fabled cloak of invisibilty which Ariadne had unraveled to make the magical thread which guided Theseus through the path to kill the monstrous bull-headed creature which was the son of Akama's grandmother P'sephae. Now it was rewoven again on the loom of Athena.

"It will cover two, but barely," said Ariadne. "Posudi can see through it if he's aware that it's being used but he's not all-knowing; he can't watch every ship. He relies on lesser beings, the Wild Ones of the Sea, to bring him news, and they can see through it no more than mortals can. Don't take an obvious ship. Posudi might take a look himself at any ship sent by Nestor that seemed to be heading for Kaphtu, no matter how innocent it looked. Call on us if necessary, but we have a great deal of confidence in the two of you. Blessings."

She was gone, and we were staring at Akama's hands as if we could see the invisible veil they held. "It's all very well for her to say don't take an obvious ship," I began.

Akama's lovely eyes took on a familiar look of calculation. "I wonder," said my devious darling, "if that Argive ship that brought the embassy to Nestor has left yet..."

It hadn't, and that led to the most uncomfortable sea voyage I have ever taken. Young Antilochus was taken enough into our confidence to be a great deal of help to us. He was enough of a boy still to regard it all as an enormous joke. By pretending to be sympathetic to the Argives he easily gained their confidence—

getting the Prince of Pylos on the Argive side would make up for their failure to enlist Nestor's aid, at least to some extent. He learned that when they left Pylos they would sail directly for Kaphtu, meeting the other Argive raiders on the way.

A word from Antilochus to Nestor when we were ready to move and the Argive envoys were told that they had overstayed their welcome. They prepared to sail and Antilochus came to bid them farewell, bringing aboard two unseen visitors, myself and Akama under the Veil of Adis. Then Antilochus set off on a visit to some nearby relatives, taking with him in his chariot two of our sailors from Kaphtu. One, who resembled me slightly, wore clothing of mine, and the other, the smallest and slightest of our group, muffled himself in Akama's cloak. It was unconventional to take a woman on such a visit, but the people of Pylos had gotten used to the un-Danaan freedom of Akama and the close friendship between Akama and me and young Antilochus. Until Antilochus returned from his journey with an explanation for his parents' ears only, we would not be missed at the palace of Nestor and Anaxibia.

We were aboard the ship, then, and heading for Kaphtu. The trouble was that there is not much room on any ship and even less on a ship of war. There were very few places during the day where we could rest in any comfort, and if we settled down to sleep at night we had scant comfort and a constant worry that some member of the crew would stumble over us. And fond as we were of each other, the necessity to stay constantly close enough so that the Veil of Adis covered us both grew irksome. The Veil seemed to inhibit the need for food or sleep, but I was not sure that it was wise for us to stay under it the whole voyage. Akama and I took turns slipping out of the Veil in some hidden corner for rest and food while the other, hidden by the Veil, kept guard. We lived like the mice in a poor man's house, constantly on the alert and never getting proper food or comfortable rest.

Eventually we joined the Argive fleet, hidden near one of the less inhabited Circle Islands, and knew that in one long day's voyage we would be off the shores of Kaphtu. Our last night was the most uncomfortable of all, for when the fleet made the landfall off the coast of Kaphtu it hove to and maintained its position with oars until dawn. Men were constantly moving about the dark ship and we were almost discovered a dozen times.

From eavesdropping on the ship's officers, we knew that the Argive plan was to land near the old palace of M'lia which had never been rebuilt after the Great Wave. They planned to land their forces, circle around N'sos and attack it from the landward side. It was not a bad plan, though I think that they would have been discovered by our watchposts before getting very far and ambushed before they got to N'sos. As it turned out, I had no chance to see whether the land defenses of Kaphtu would have been able to deal with them.

The landing was planned to begin at first light. The Argive fleet, which had kept in contact through the night by lantern signals, carefully shaded so as not to be seen from shore, gathered around the ships of the

principal Argive captains and swept toward the shore
at the best speed their rowers could manage. The
Argive leaders had evidently decided that their fleet
was too big to be concealed and had decided on a
speedy rather than a stealthy approach.

Akama and I were standing at the stern of the ship
in the clear space on the rail opposite where the
steersman stood. The steersman was not a sociable
man, we discovered, and when he himself was
steering, this space was likely to be clear. He stood
there himself when his apprentice was at the steering
oar, but for this last dash to the beach he himself took
the oar and the apprentice was lending a hand
somewhere else. So we had as good a view as the
steersman had, and that necessarily had to be a good
one. The captain of the ship, with a few of his officers
around him, stood at the front of the afterdeck, only a
few paces away from us.

The beach, still littered with stones and debris that
had never been cleared after the Great Wave, came
closer and closer. As the sun came over the hills on the
headland to the east of the deserted beach it
illuminated the scene with a harsh light, casting long
shadows from every stone and bush. Far down the
beach to the west there was a flash of bronze and I
heard the captain swear, "Cast them down to Hades, I
think the Cretan bull-lovers have had warning of our
coming and are going to make us fight for the beach.
Archers down there—string your bows. Heavily armed
men—don't disembark until we're in really shallow
water. Oarsmen—I want her driven right up on the
beach."

It was no force of Kaphtui coast guards that was coming up the beach faster than a horse could run but a gigantic man taller than a tree, seemingly made of solid bronze, but bronze that cold bend and flex like flesh. Our ship had the misfortune to be on the left flank and one of the nearest ships to shore. As the bronze giant came to the point on the beach nearest us, he picked up a massive rock from the beach as easily as I would pick up a jar of wine and hurled it at us with deadly aim. It hit the oars on one side of the ship. They snapped like straws and I heard screams from oarsmen as the butts of the snapped oars were torn from their hands to wreak havoc in the rowers' benches.

The captain was a hardened sea raider, but he was deadly pale and his voice had a quaver he could not control as he shouted, "Back! Stand to what oars are left and get us away from this cursed shore!" The crew, veterans of many a fight, though none so strange as this, managed to get some way on the ship, and Akama and I saw the shores of our homeland begin to recede, as the frantic sea raiders tried to get out of range of the monster's missiles.

Chapter Eighteen
THE PROPHECY

I had no desire to be carried back to the Argolid, or indeed to spend any more time on that ship. I whispered to Akama—I might just as well have shouted for all the attention any crewman had to spare—"Over the rail, hang by your hands till you see a chance to jump, then swim for your life to clear the oars." As soon as she was over the rail I whipped off the Veil of Adis and tied it around my waist. As I prepared to dive clear, one of the officers on the bridge saw me appear and turned pale with shock. He laid a hand to his sword but as I whipped the Veil round my waist making it look as if I were cut into two pieces his knees buckled and he gaped at me helplessly as I made a long dive to clear the frantically moving oars.

I knew that Akama was as good a swimmer as I and I wasted no time in looking for her but swam for the beach at top speed. By luck, I was almost on her heels as she scrambled out of the water. A great wave caused by one of the giant's missiles nearly sucked us both back into the sea but I hurled myself on top of Akama and we both clawed for any kind of handhold on the beach. The wave didn't quite dislodge us, and, bruised and battered, we crawled up the beach to the shelter of a stone too large for even the giant to lift. With my last strength I unwrapped the Veil of Adis from my waist and threw it over us.

Gasping and spitting out water, we lay back against the stone and watched the scene near the beach. At first the giant merely threw stones near the ships or at their

189

oars. Made bold by this, some Argive leader rallied a group of ships and they drove at the giant in a ragged wedge, shooting arrows and hurling spears as they hove within range. The giant waded toward the ship. The missiles rattled off his bronze skin as spray bounces off a ship's prow. As the lead ship reached him with madly brave Argive warriors leaning out to hack at him with swords or axes or poke at him with spears, the giant put one mighty hand on the ship's prow and lifted the bow of the ship clean out of the water, so that her crew began to slide toward the stern, dropping their weapons to cling frantically to any handhold. The giant gave a tremendous shove and the ship shot out to sea as if her sails were full of a gale-force wind.

He waded waist deep into the sea to give two other Argive ships the same mighty shove. One battle-maddened captain drew his ship alongside the half-submerged giant, with every crewman trying to find a chink in the monster's defenses with sword, axe, spear or arrow. The giant grabbed its mast with one titanic hand and, with first sign of effort it had shown so far, literally pushed the ship under water as I might submerge a bucket to fill it. The mast broke off in his hand. He changed grip and hurled it like a spear at a large ship which was standing out of range. The flung mast hit inside the ship and went through her bottom. The ship began to fill and sink.

One last ship attempted to ram him. He swatted it like a fly with one massive hand and it flew to pieces like a smashed pot. It was the last attack. I think the large ship he had holed with the mast may have been the flagship and when it was sunk there was no one to rally the attack again. The giant returned to the shore, water streaming from his bronze skin, and began throwing rocks again.

I was gripping Akama so tightly that she had to ask me to loosen my hold, and her voice brought me out of a sort of fascinated trance. I spoke to her in a low voice. "Do you notice that he doesn't attack men directly, and unless they attack him only tries to drive them off? And he's not throwing stones at ships that stand in only to pick up swimmers."

She nodded, but her voice was somber. "Plenty of men were killed, nonetheless, drowned when the ships sank or crushed when he smashed their ships. I hope there's no need for more of this."

It seemed not at the moment. The Argive fleet, having picked up all the swimmers they could find, was limping slowly out to sea. The first of the winter winds, which had held off till now, was raising whitecaps on the ocean.

"I don't envy them their voyage home," I said. "I'm glad we didn't have to give Kaphtui lives to fight them off, but they were brave men. We should see that any bodies washed ashore have decent burial."

There was a crunch of sand near us and a shadow fell over us. The bronze giant had stridden up the beach as I talked, and now he stood still, moving his head like a hound casting for a scent. Close to, I could see that his face and form were manlike, but crude and massive like those of an archaic statue.

Evidently he could not see through the Veil of Adis, but suddenly I had little taste for cowering like a

191

rabbit as he hunted the beach for the voice he must have heard. Before Akama could stop me I slipped out from under the Veil of Adis and stood at his feet, throwing my head back to look into the face high above me. "In the name of the Lord Apollo," I said, "I greet you. I am Ducalion, M'nos of Kaphtu. And you, I think, must be here because of a pledge Apollo gave me."

I stood there wondering if he had any intelligence or only a blind hostility and would smash me as he had smashed the ships. His face moved, not down to me but up toward the sky, and he stood for a moment as though listening to a voice. Then his mighty bulk moved toward me. I took a step back involuntarity, but the monstrous creature was kneeling, like a slave, on one knee, back bent and giant head looming above mine. A deep booming voice spoke with a muted roar; the creature was evidently making an effort not to deafen me.

"I am Talos, lord," he boomed. "For my alloted span I must patrol your coasts and let no enemy set foot on Kaphtu. The Lord Apollo asks, are you paid for your journey?"

I tried to keep relief out of my voice as I said. "Well paid, Talos. Do not frighten my people more than you can help and repel invaders as you did today with as little loss of life as you can. I thank you for your guardianship."

There was no expression in that muted boom replied, "No thanks are due me. I also am under obligation. But your words are gracious and your commands wise, M'nos of the Kaphtui. I wish you and your land well." Then he was on his feet again striding off down the beach. As he reached the headland his brazen voice gave a great challenging shout that must have made the fleeing Argives bend to their oars.

Akama emerged from the Veil of Adis with her eyes flashing. "Fool," she said. But she grabbed me and kissed me with a passion that took away the sting of the word. Then she leaned against me wearily. I thought at first I might have to carry her to the nearest settlement, but she reached into the same reserves of strength that had made her a great Leaper, and straightened her weary body. She pulled her fingers through the tangles in her still-wet hair and smiled wryly as she looked at me, as soaked and scraped and weary as she was herself. "The King and Queen of Kaphtu are home," she said. Her eyes turned to the wind-whipped sea. "Somehow I don't think we'll go voyaging again for awhile."

I tried to make my stunned mind work. "I know the palace at M'lia is abandoned now," I said, "but surely there must be a village somewhere near." We trudged up the beach looking for a path up the cliffs and eventually found the remnants of the old road from the beach to the abandoned palace. As we came over the crest, we could see a group of soldiers coming toward us, led by a young man who looked like a palace official, perhaps, I thought, the local administrator.

I had thought that we would have to identify ourselves and even establish our identity, but as soon as he saw us the young man who seemed to be the leader of the group called out, "Praise to Zeus, Protector of Travelers! M'nos Ducalion and Ariadne

Akama are restored to us." They gave us the military salute, swords drawn and presented before their faces. Soldiers call it "kissing the blade," and it is a salute given only to a high commander.

The young man who seemed to be their leader came toward us. "All will be well in Kaphtu now that you are back among your people," he said.

I shook my head wearily. "Not all," I replied. "How is the land? Is the blight still bad?"

His voice came back with a strange trace of familiarity. "Bad and will be worse before it's better. But all will come well in the end. Zeus will not let the people starve for one goddess's wrath."

I looked at him, wondering how he knew of such matters and suddenly a suspicion began to grow in my mind. His voice seemed to deepen as he went on. "Rest now and be secure, Ducalion, M'nos of Kaphtu; and Akama, Ariadne of Kaphtu. Your borders are secure and you need mix no more in the affairs of the Olympians. Children will come to you and other things your hearts desire. The days of Kaphtu as a great empire are done, but it will be a peaceful and bountiful land, governed with justice and wisdom. You will live long and prosper."

As I looked into those familiar/ unfamiliar eyes, I knew that his prophecies would come true, for he was, after all, the god of prophecy. As I said at the beginning of my story, I can always tell an Olympian.

About the Author

Richard Purtill is Professor Emeritus of Philosophy at Western Washington University, and the author of nineteen published books, including six fantasy and science fiction novels. He has made more than twenty visits to Greece, and lived several years in England. His stories have been published in The Magazine of Fantasy and Science Fiction, Isaac Asimov's Science Fiction Magazine, Marion Zimmer Bradley's Fantasy Magazine, Alfred Hitchcock's Mystery Magazine, and The Year's Best Fantasy Stories.

He is a popular presenter at conferences and conventions, and has been guest of honor at Mythcon in San Diego. He is a member of Science Fiction and Fantasy Writers of America, the Author's Guild, and the National Writer's Union.

Made in the USA
Columbia, SC
29 January 2022

55014629R00113